Reckless !

GUNS N' ROSES

a Graphic Novel

JIM McCARTHY
MARC OLIVENT

This edition published by Omnibus Press and distributed in the United States and Canada by
The Overlook Press, Peter Mayer Publishers Inc, 141 Wooster Street, New York, NY 10012. For bulk
and special sales requests, please contact sales@overlookny.com or write to us at the above address.

Copyright © 2015 Omnibus Press
(A Division of Music Sales Limited)
14/15 Berners Street,
London, W1T 3LJ, UK.

Cover illustrated by Marc Olivent
Text by Jim McCarthy
Book illustrated by Marc Olivent

ISBN 978.1.4683.1139.6

Printed in Croatia.

A catalogue record for this book is available from the British Library.

Cataloguing-in-Publication data is available from the Library of Congress.

Visit Omnibus Press on the web at www.omnibuspress.com

Reckless Life
GUNS N' ROSES

a Graphic Novel

JIM McCARTHY
MARC OLIVENT

OVERLOOK OMNIBUS

Introduction

I'm writing this introduction in 2015, which happens to mark 30 years since Guns N'Roses formed in Los Angeles, 28 since they released perhaps the greatest rock album of the 1980s and 18 since they became, for all intents and purposes, a singer plus hired hands. But it doesn't matter if you're reading this in 2020, or 2050, or (assuming World War Three hasn't "done an Axl" on us) even further into the future: the fact remains, and will always remain, that for a fleetingly brief period of time, Guns N'Roses made some incredibly exciting music, defining a generation in doing so.

In *Reckless Life: The Guns N'Roses Graphic*, Jim McCarthy and Marc Olivent demonstrate exactly what it was that made Axl, Slash, Izzy, Duff and Steven (plus their replacements) such a vital force before too much fame and too many psychological issues blew them apart. There's a reason why artists as disparate as Sheryl Crow and the Manic Street Preachers continue to sing the praises of a band whose roots and musical style are so far removed from their own: it's because the musicians' tortured backgrounds and multifarious influences were channelled, brilliantly, into universally compelling music.

At first, anyway.

One of the reasons why *Reckless Life: The Guns N'Roses Graphic* works so well is because it shows us, in relentless monochrome, how GNR rose so spectacularly and fell so fast. It's the classic arc which we biographers love so much because it gives our books shape and purpose, although few bands flew so close to the sun or crashed with so much devastation as this one.

(That is assuming you regard the current Guns N'Roses as a failed entity: dear old Axl is still treading the boards with his gang of merry men and the terrible songs which appeared on the *Chinese Democracy* album, and getting well paid for it, too.)

Why so much talk of Axl, the mercurial singer? Read the opening pages of this book. His background in Lafayette, Indiana, was truly miserable from the ground up, beginning with crippling confusion about what his name actually was. What does that do to a kid, especially when you add in liberal doses of those societal ills, domestic violence and religious dogma? In this kid's case, it fills him with the drive to get the hell out, move to the city, adopt a new name and, for the next decade or so, become the most effervescent voice in hard rock.

But we're not disregarding the influences of the other players on this insane stage. We also take a close look at Slash, born Saul Hudson in Stoke-on-Trent – in many ways the polar opposite environment to Hollywood, where GNR first coalesced; Izzy Stradlin, Axl's childhood friend; Duff McKagan, the Seattle punk whose clear vision led him to morph into a Los Angeles glam-metaller; and Steven Adler, who got Slash into the guitar and – of all these lost souls – embraced the rock'n'roll lifestyle most, paying an appropriate price for his decisions. Together the fatal fivesome came up with *Appetite For Destruction*, the quintessential 'LA metal' record, released in 1987, the year which Slash later called "the most 80s year of the 80s".

You probably know *Appetite* pretty well, if you're reading this – but if you haven't heard it for a while, go and listen to it again. The sheer, breathtaking confidence – no, arrogance – of the album is still hard to grasp. Sure, the slick reek of Aerosmith and the New York Dolls is all over the riffs, but those vocals, arrangements and solos are GNR's and GNR's alone. It's their masterpiece.

Slide forward a few years and we're into the *Use Your Illusion* era. A huge transformation had taken place, with the former street urchins evolved into a massive corporate entity. For all intents and purposes, when Guns N'Roses co-headlined one of the biggest tours ever alongside Metallica in 1992, they peaked: nothing they or any other band might do nowadays – in these cash-strapped times for the music industry – is likely to top it. And yet that tour was full of negativity, with Axl making the audience wait hours before he'd appear (Metallica wisely went on stage first) and the support act Faith No More likening the tour to an unpleasant day job.

Members had come and gone, too: FNM keyboard player Roddy Bottum said at the time, "I'm getting more and more confused about who's in Guns N'Roses. There's Dizzy and Iggy and Lizzy and Tizzy and Gilbey and Giddy... shit man, onstage now there's a horn section, two chick backup singers, two keyboard players, an airplane pilot, a basketball coach, a couple of car mechanics..."

Which sums up Guns N'Roses' fall from grace rather well. Losing focus, forced more and more to bow to Axl's demands and aware that their music was less compelling in the switched-on late 1990s, the original musicians slipped away, leaving the band more or less on hiatus for a decade while the singer decided what to do next. By 2000 Guns N'Roses were just about Axl, as this book displays so well, right up to his 2012 appearance on Jimmy Kimmel's ABC talk show.

What are we left with? Some of the most visceral music of a generation, and a clear, penetrating depiction of where it all went right and where it all went wrong. In *Reckless Life: The Guns N'Roses Graphic* you get to see it all at the sharp end of an artist's pencil, complete with quotes from the players themselves. The ups and downs of those heady days of the late 80s and early 90s will not come again, for Guns N'Roses or for any of us – but this book will give you an illuminating picture of these talented, doomed musicians which is as close as you'll get to actually being there.

Joel McIver, 2015
www.joelmciver.co.uk

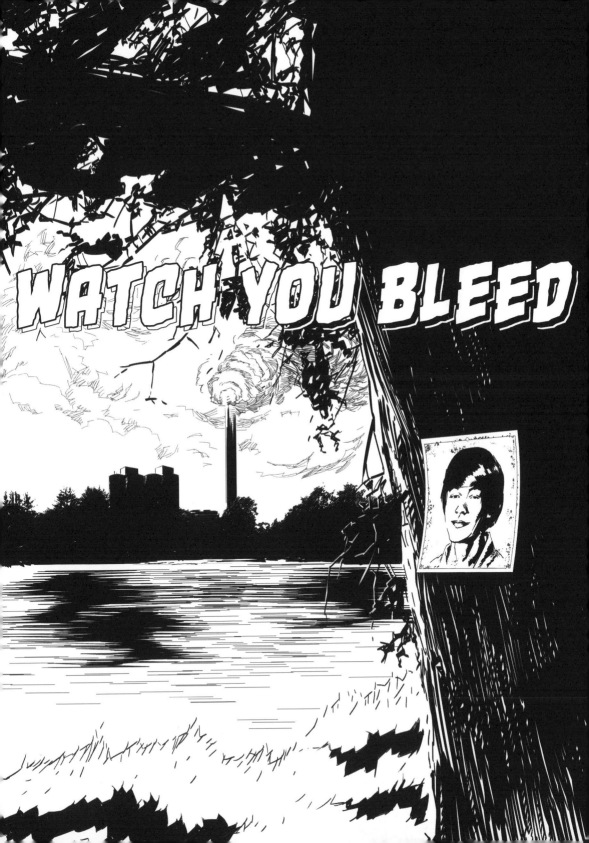

...BLUE-COLLAR RELIGIOSITY...

...DURNED RELIGIOSITY DONE AND GONE AND DROVE A POOR BOY MAD...

...INSTEAD OF THE LOVE, WE GOT THE RELIGION...

...A RECIPE FOR DISASTER EMOTIONALLY, MENTALLY AND SPIRITUALLY...

DID I MENTION BLUE-COLLAR RELIGIOSITY?

I'M A PENTECOSTAL BOY... I WAS BROUGHT UP *REAL* PENTECOSTAL... BUT THIS WAS NOT LIKE THE FIRST DAY OF PENTECOST. THIS IS MORE ABOUT *RULES AND REGULATIONS* AND *CONFORMING* AND *STRICT RELIGION* WITH NO LOVE AT *ALL*, MAN.

COLOSSIANS 3:19, NIV... HUSBANDS, LOVE YOUR WIVES AND DO NOT BE HARSH WITH THEM...

WATCHING THE SO-CALLED RELIGIOUS ADULTS AROUND ME, THEIR WAY OF BEHAVING AND THEIR WAY OF BEING...

..WITH DAD JUST SUDDENLY BAILING OUT OF OUR HOME... Y'KNOW, JUST LIKE THAT...

AND THAT WAS IT, HE JUST GONE GOT UP AND LEFT...

INSTEAD OF THE HOLY DOVE, WE GOT THE RULES AND THE MAN-MADE REGULATIONS...

WE GOT THE STRAITJACKET AND NOT THE FREEDOM...

...IT SURE WORKED REAL WELL FOR ME...

The Bible

THE TV IN OUR LIVING ROOM WAS THE GODDAM DEVIL WRIT LARGE.

IT WAS THE CROUCHING BEAST IN THE CORNER, THROWING OFF WEIRD SHAPES AND STRANGE LIGHT...

...GUESS SATAN JUST WALKED IN AND ENTERED THE HOUSE... AT LEAST FOR A HOT WHILE... BACK IN ANOTHER OF HIS OWN HELLS... JUST LIKE MY HOME REALLY... A VERSION OF HELL... ONE THAT WAS MADE ESPECIALLY FOR US AND US ALONE...

FAST FORWARD TO 1988. WE'RE AT THE RITZ, LOS ANGELES...

FIVE OR SIX YEARS AGO, I HITCHHIKED HERE AND ENDED UP STUCK OUT IN THIS PLACE... CLIMBED UP THE RAMP OUTTA THE FREEWAY AND THIS BLACK MAN COMES UP TO MY FRIEND AND ME AND US WITH JUST ABOUT TEN BUCKS BETWEEN US... HE SCREAMED AT US...

MAN!!! DO YOU KNOW WHERE YOU ARE?

YOU IN THE JUNGLE BABEE...

AND YOU GONNA DIEEE...

LIVE AT THE RITZ

I WONDER, IF WE COULD SEE INTO THE FUTURE, WHAT WOULD WE REALLY DO? WOULD WE GRAB IT OR WOULD WE RUN FROM IT LIKE HELL?

...SO WELCOME TO THE JUNGLE...

MATTHEW 18:1-6... AT THAT TIME THE DISCIPLES CAME TO JESUS, SAYING, "WHO IS THE GREATEST IN THE KINGDOM OF HEAVEN?" AND CALLING TO HIM A CHILD, HE PUT HIM IN THE MIDST OF THEM AND SAID, "TRULY, I SAY TO YOU, UNLESS YOU TURN AND BECOME LIKE CHILDREN, YOU WILL NEVER ENTER THE KINGDOM OF HEAVEN. WHOEVER HUMBLES HIMSELF LIKE THIS CHILD IS THE GREATEST IN THE KINGDOM OF HEAVEN...

WHOEVER RECEIVES ONE SUCH CHILD IN MY NAME RECEIVES ME, BUT WHOEVER CAUSES ONE OF THESE LITTLE ONES WHO BELIEVE IN ME TO SIN, IT WOULD BE BETTER FOR HIM TO HAVE A GREAT MILLSTONE FASTENED AROUND HIS NECK AND TO BE DROWNED IN THE DEPTH OF THE SEA...

LET'S FAST-FORWARD AGAIN, SHALL WE?

I AM BEING GIVEN, OR I SHOULD SAY I AM UNDERTAKING, SOME PAST LIFE REGRESSION HERE...

EVER SINCE I WAS SEVENTEEN YEARS OLD AND FOUND OUT ABOUT MY 'BIOLOGICAL' FATHER, I HAVE HAD THIS ITCH INSIDE ME... LIKE A DEMON CLAWING AT MY INSIDES.

I AM DREDGING SHIT UP FROM MY SUBCONSCIOUS... OR IS IT MY CONSCIOUS? AFTER FINDING OUT AT AGE SEVENTEEN ABOUT MY REAL FATHER AND HIS ABUSE... IT WAS AROUND THEN THAT I CHANGED MY NAME TO W. ROSE.

I THEN BECAME AXL ROSE COMPLETELY ABOUT FOUR YEARS LATER... AND NOT LONG AFTER I WAS IN THE BAND AXL....

THE STEPFATHER WAS NEXT IN LINE TOO... WITH MORE ABUSE FOR ME AND MY SIBLINGS... LIKE THEY ARE ALL JUST WAITING IN LINE...

DON'T YOU SEE THAT WHATEVER ENTERS THE MOUTH GOES INTO THE STOMACH AND THEN OUT OF THE BODY? BUT THE THINGS THAT COME OUT OF A PERSON'S MOUTH COME FROM THE HEART, AND THESE DEFILE THEM...

FOR OUT OF THE HEART COMES EVIL THOUGHTS: MURDER, ADULTERY, SEXUAL IMMORALITY, THEFT, FALSE TESTIMONY, SLANDER. THESE ARE WHAT DEFILE A PERSON. MATTHEW: 17-20.

DID I DRINK FROM THE CUP OF WRATH?

I FEEL LIKE I'M DROWNING HERE...

I NEED TO GO... TO GET OUT OF HERE *REAL SOON* BEFORE IT'S *TOO LATE*... I'M DROWNING ALIVE IN LAFAYETTE...

ANOTHER YOUNG GUY WITH PLENTY OF ATTITUDE WAS HANGING AROUND LAFAYETTE...

HE WAS SPORTING AN ATTITUDE AND A KEITH RICHARDS FIXATION AND HE HAD *THE LOOK*.

MY NAME IS *IZZY STRADLIN*, OR THAT'S WHAT I CAME TO BE CALLED... MAYBE I SHOULD TELL YOU MY REAL NAME A LITTLE LATER...

IT WAS COOL GROWING UP IN LAFAYETTE. THERE'S A COURTHOUSE, A COLLEGE, A RIVER AND SOME RAILROAD TRACKS...

IT'S A SMALL TOWN, SO THERE WASN'T MUCH TO DO. WE RODE BIKES, SMOKED POT, GOT INTO A LITTLE TROUBLE... IT WAS PRETTY BEAVIS AND BUTT-HEAD ACTUALLY...

IT'S FUNNY HOW FIVE DISPARATE GUYS FROM DIFFERENT TOWNS OR DIFFERENT CITIES CONVERGED AND CAME TO MAKE A BIG DIFFERENCE TO MUSIC HISTORY.

ALL WE DID WAS TAKE A CHANCE... A BIG CHANCE... HOW COULD ANY OF US HAVE KNOWN?

ME AND WILLIAM BAILEY WERE LONG-HAIRED GUYS IN HIGH SCHOOL...

YOU WERE EITHER A JOCK OR A STONER. WE WEREN'T JOCKS, SO WE ENDED UP HANGING OUT TOGETHER.

WE'D PLAY COVERS IN THE GARAGE... THERE WERE NO CLUBS TO PLAY AT, SO WE NEVER MADE IT OUT OF THE GARAGE...

BIG IDEAS IN A VERY SMALL TOWN... NOW THOSE BIG IDEAS WERE COMING FROM TWO DREAMERS COMBINED... WITH EVEN *BIGGER IDEAS*...

BACK THEN I KNEW HIM AS WILLIAM BRUCE BAILEY... LATER ON HE WOULD BECOME WHO WE NOW KNOW AS *AXL ROSE*...

...LASHED ON, WITH SOME WEIRD ADULT
...OING ON, WHEN I WAS A YOUNG KID...

MY MOM STARTED WORKING PROFESSIONALLY WITH *DAVID BOWIE*. I'M PRETTY SURE THAT'S HOW IT STARTED AND THEN IT TURNED INTO SOME SORT OF MYSTERIOUS ROMANCE THAT WENT ON FOR A WHILE AFTER THAT. BOWIE WAS ALWAYS OVER AND THEY WERE ALWAYS TOGETHER...

SSSSSHHH! I CAUGHT THEM *NAKED* ONCE. THEY HAD A LOT OF STUFF GOING ON, BUT MY PERSPECTIVE AT TEN WAS LIMITED... LOOKING BACK ON IT, I KNEW EXACTLY WHAT WAS GOING ON.

LOS ANGELES, CALIFORNIA.

THINGS CHANGED AND FAST. MOM AND DAD SEPARATED AND THEN THEY GOT DIVORCED. I KINDA WENT OFF THE RAILS AROUND THEN... I DRANK, I USED DRUGS AND I ACTED OUT...

I STAYED WITH MY GRAN, OLA SENIOR, AS MOM WENT AWAY A LOT TO WORK AND MAKE MONEY TO SUPPORT US...

I GOT INTO THE US EDUCATIONAL STREAM AT AN ELEMENTARY SCHOOL, THEN MOVED UP TO BANCROFT JUNIOR HIGH SCHOOL. I WAS FOURTEEN AND I STILL HAD NOT CONNECTED WITH THE GUITAR, BUT THAT WAS TO COME SOON...

I WAS STILL HANGING OUT AT THIS ELEMENTARY SCHOOL BECAUSE THEY HAD THESE HALF-PIPE BANKS -- I USED TO BE INTO FREESTYLE ON BICYCLES -- AND THERE WAS THIS KID WHO HAD FALLEN OFF HIS SKATEBOARD... I THOUGHT HE HAD KILLED HIMSELF. I WENT OVER TO SEE IF HE WAS ALRIGHT AND WE STARTED HANGING OUT AFTER THAT.

'HIS NAME WAS STEVEN 'POPCORN' ADLER AND HE WAS TO FIGURE IN MY LIFE BIG TIME LATER ON.

I LOVED SKATEBOARDS AND THEN I GOT REAL BIKE CRAZY... THAT WAS MY BIG OBSESSION FOR A WHILE...

I LOVED BIKE MOTOCROSS AND BMX... BUT STEVIE POPCORN WAS CERTAINLY NO SIDEWALK SURFER, THAT'S FO' SURE...

MY BUDDY POPCORN AND ME WERE HANGING OUT AND I STARTED TO DEVELOP A TASTE FOR STEALING.

IN OTHERS WORDS, I BECAME A REAL KLEPTO-MANIAC...

STEVE HAD A GUITAR AT HIS GRANDMOTHER'S PLACE IN HOLLYWOOD WHERE HE WAS STAYING...

I WAS SOON LOGGING IN UP TO TWELVE HOURS A DAY ON THE FRETBOARD...

I GOT SERIOUS ABOUT GETTING MY CHOPS DOWN...

STEVE USED TO PLAY *KISS* SONGS... ACTUALLY HE COULDN'T PLAY *ANYTHING*, BUT IT WAS A HUGE TURN ON FOR HIM... AND FOR *ME* TOO, JUST WATCHING HIM...

THE REASON WE WERE AT MY GRANDMOTHER'S IS I GOT UNCEREMONIOUSLY TOSSED OUT OF MY HOME WHEN I WAS ONLY THIRTEEN YEARS OLD. MY PEOPLE WERE OUT OF CLEVELAND, OHIO AND I WAS BORN OUT THERE ON JANUARY 22ND 1965...

I GREW UP IN THE *SAN FERNANDO VALLEY* UNTIL, AT THE AGE OF THIRTEEN, I WAS SENT TO LIVE WITH MY GRANDPARENTS IN *HOLLYWOOD* DUE TO MY BAD BEHAVIOUR.

AFTER NINTH GRADE, I RETURNED TO MY PARENTS' HOUSE IN THE VALLEY FOR THE REMAINDER OF HIGH SCHOOL. THEN I STARTED LEARNING TO PLAY DRUMS...

A SUPER BAD GUY JUST SEEMED TO COME UP OUT OF ME WHEN I WAS A WEE YOUNGSTER. I WAS REALLY BAD... I GOT THROWN OUT OF *EIGHT* OR *NINE* DIFFERENT SCHOOLS...

I USED TO FIGHT WITH THE TEACHERS. I'D GET IN A FIGHT EVERY DAY... I WAS JUST A FEISTY LITTLE KID...

MY OTHER MEMORIES OF MY DAD TONY ARE ALL CINEMATIC REALLY, LOOKING UP TO HIM AND WALKING EVERYWHERE IN LOS ANGELES...

I MEAN, NO ONE WALKS *ANYWHERE* IN LA.

ON ONE OF THESE WALKS HE TOLD ME THAT HIM AND MOM WERE SEPARATING. I WAS DEVASTATED, MAN...

I WAS FIFTEEN YEARS OLD WHEN I FOUND A SHITTY OLD BEAT-UP GUITAR IN MY GRANDMA'S HOUSE...

BY THEN WE HAD MOVED TO RANGELY DRIVE AND IT WAS EXCITING, I GUESS... LIKE I SAID, BOWIE WAS AROUND THEN...

BMX WAS REALLY HAPPENING AND
MY GRAN BOUGHT ME A *WEBCO BIKE.*

PEOPLE HAD
TO GET OUTTA OUR WAY...
WE WOULD RIDE ANYWHERE...
OVER *FIRE HYDRANTS...*
OVER *BUS STOP BENCHES,*
JUST WEAVING IN AND OUT
OF THE TRAFFIC
ALL OVER.

WE TREATED THE STREETS AS OUR BIKE PARK...
FROM *LA BREA TAR PITS* TO *CULVER CITY* TO THE
VALLEY IN *RESEDA...* WE GOT ALL THE WAY OUT
THERE AND *RESEDA* WAS A GOOD *FIFTEEN MILES*
FROM *HOLLYWOOD...* SO WE WERE BEING *REAL*
AMBITIOUS...

MEANWHILE, *HOLLYWOOD* WAS A
GREAT PLACE TO GRAB A RIDE ON
THE BACK OR THE TAILGATE OF A
CAR... WE'D BE HITTING UP TO
FORTY MILES AN HOUR...

YOU TRY THIS... HANGING ON FOR DEAR LIFE AROUND THE TWISTS AND TURNS OF LAUREL CANYON.

MY FRIENDS THOUGHT I WAS SUPER COOL WITH MY DARING STUNTS...

WE HUNG OUT AT LAUREL ELEMENTARY SCHOOL AND RODE IN THEIR PLAYGROUND.

THE PRINCIPAL WAS GETTING FURIOUS... WE WERE WRECKING THE PLACE.

I DIDN'T *GIVE* A SHIT. MY PARENTS SPLITTING UP TOOK A *BIG TOLL* ON ME. I JUST DIDN'T GIVE A *FUCK* ANYMORE...

THERE WERE SOME GREAT CHARACTERS AROUND. *MIKE BALZARY (AKA FLEA),* WHO WENT ON TO FAME WITH THE *RED HOT CHILI PEPPERS,* WAS HANGING AROUND. HE'D PLAY A LITTLE TRUMPET AND BIKE WITH US ALL.

HOLLYWOOD

WE COULD HEAR 'EM COMING, BUT IT WAS TOO LATE, MAN...

WE GOT NABBED ALRIGHT... BUT I WAS PRACTICALLY LAUGHING IN THEIR FACES, DUDE...

wREEEEEOOOOOO

THE COPS REALLY HASSLED US, BUT AS TWELVE-YEAR-OLDS, WE DIDN'T HAVE ANY ID...

I AIN'T TELLING YOU *NOTHING*, MAN... AND I AIN'T *SCARED* OF YOU EITHER...

OKAY THEN, MY NAME IS *MICHAEL MOUSE*. YEAH, THAT'S RIGHT...

I WAS ALWAYS GETTING IN TROUBLE AROUND THEN... BUT THEY HAD TO *CATCH* ME FIRST AND MOST TIMES THEY WEREN'T *SMART* OR *QUICK* ENOUGH TO DO SO.

HEY YOU, *MOTHERFUCKER*, COME BACK HERE, I WANNA KICK YOUR ASS...

HEY, ASSHOLE... CATCH ME IF YOU *CAN*.

AFTER RAISING ALL OF US EIGHT KIDS, MOM GOT A JOB AT THE AGE OF FORTY-FIVE AND WENT OUT INTO THE WORLD OF FULL-TIME EMPLOYMENT.

I CAUGHT MY DAD AND OUR NEXT DOOR NEIGHBOUR'S WIFE IN BED TOGETHER WHEN I WAS ABOUT NINE YEARS OLD... FROM THAT DAY ON, I STOPPED TALKING TO MY DAD.

I HAD BEEN INTRODUCED TO THE GROWN-UP WORLD OF DECEIT, OF SEX AND OF CHEATING... I REALLY NEEDED TO HIDE THIS FROM MY MOM.

SO ANYWAY, MY DAD AND THE NEIGHBOUR'S WIFE WENT AND MOVED IN TOGETHER AND IT WAS NOT LONG AFTER THAT MY MOM AND DAD GOT THE INEVITABLE DIVORCE.

I STARTED GETTING PANIC ATTACKS AND A FEW YEARS LATER I STARTED MEDICATING WITH BOOZE AND DRUGS... TO TRY AND CALM THE INNER CHAOS AND THE TURBULENT STORMS THAT ROILED INSIDE ME...

I SURVIVED AND THAT NEAR-DEATH EVENT SHORED ME UP IN THE FUTURE WHEN I ALMOST REPEATED IT IN A VERY DIFFERENT MANNER. IN FACT, MY MOM GOT ME TO DO A STUDY ABOUT *NEAR-DEATH EXPERIENCES.* MY RECOLLECTIONS WERE FEATURED IN A BOOK CALLED *CLOSER TO THE LIGHT: LEARNING FROM THE NEAR-DEATH EXPERIENCES OF CHILDREN.*

THERE WERE MILLIONS OF BANDS AND PLACES TO PLAY... AND THAT'S BARELY AN EXAGGERATION. I PASSED THROUGH OVER THIRTY-ONE BANDS DURING MY EARLY DAYS IN SEATTLE... INCLUDING A HARDCORE PUNK BAND CALLED *THE FARTZ.*

I GOT IN THE FASTBACKS TOO, BY FALLING BACK ON MY DRUMMING SKILLS. I WAS ALSO IN *TEN MINUTE WARNING...* JUST SO MANY BANDS IN SEATTLE...

BACK THEN I WAS JUST A BROWN-HAIRED KID WHO COULDN'T MAKE UP HIS MIND WHETHER HE WANTED TO PLAY *ELECTRIC GUITAR* OR *BASS* OR *DRUMS...*

WHILE THERE WAS AN OVERABUNDANCE OF OPPORTUNITIES TO MEET OTHER MUSICIANS AND JAM, PLAYING SEATTLE CLUBS WAS ULTIMATELY A *DEAD END* FOR ANY SERIOUS MUSICIAN.

LOCATED JUST ACROSS THE STREET FROM THE PIKE PLACE MARKET, *THE SHOWBOX AT THE MARKET* WAS A GREAT SEATTLE HANGOUT... *THE GORILLA GARDENS* WAS ANOTHER GREAT PUNK-INCLINED VENUE...

SHOW BOX

20 PAPA MONK
21 ZUT ALORE
LATE FUNK NIGHT
22 ZOE FARGO
25 PANTIE CHUCKERS
27 OF MOLLY

YOU COULDN'T GET ANYWHERE, EXCEPT FOR *QUEENSRYCHE,* WHO GOT SIGNED... BUT, FOR ME, SEATTLE WAS A GOOD TRAINING GROUND.

IT WAS 1984 AND IT WAS TIME TO LEAVE TOWN. I HAD $360 TO MY NAME AND I HAD MY RIDE, WHICH WAS A 1971 FORD MAVERICK... I THINK I BOUGHT IT FOR 300 BUCKS.

I GOT PULLED OVER DRIVING LIKE CRAZY TO TRY AND CATCH BILLY IDOL ON THE TONIGHT SHOW WITH JOHNNY CARSON. I MADE SURE I HAD A COPPER PENNY HIDDEN IN MY MOUTH TO THROW OFF THE IMPENDING BREATHALYZER... WE WERE AS DRUNK AS SKUNKS...

SIR, IS THERE ANY REASON FOR YOUR RECKLESS HASTE?

OFFICER, WE WERE ONLY SPEEDING 'COS WE CAN'T MISS BILLY IDOL ON CARSON...

GODDAM IT! I NEARLY PISSED MY PANTS LAUGHING AT THIS DUDE HERE. I WAS SO ZONKED OUT OF MY MIND, MAN...

I ALSO GOT IN ANOTHER SEATTLE-BASED BAND CALLED TEN MINUTE WARNING. WE TOURED THE NORTHWEST WITH THE GREAT VANCOUVER PUNK BAND D.O.A.

I GOT BACK FROM THE TOUR AND STACY WAS GETTING INVOLVED WITH ANOTHER GUY, WHO WAS IN A SHADY CROWD DABBLING IN DRUGS. IT SURE LOOKED LIKE SHE WAS HEADING DOWN THE SMACK ROAD. SO IT WAS GOODBYE STACY AND MY FIRST REAL LOVE OF THE HEART...

10 MINUTE WARNING

ZOOM!

I WATCHED MY ROOMMATE AND GOOD BUDDY EDDY GET INTO HEROIN TOO... HE JUST SLIPPED AWAY. IT WAS A HEARTBREAKER, MAN.

I HAD TO DISTANCE MYSELF FROM THAT SCENE AND STAY FOCUSED ON MUSIC... IT SEEMED LIKE MY ONLY HOPE AND MY BIGGEST CHANCE TO MAKE A CHANGE.

OVER A TWO-YEAR PERIOD BILL BAILEY SPENT A TOTAL OF TEN DAYS IN COUNTY JAIL CHARGED WITH PUBLIC INTOXICATION, BATTERY, CONTRIBUTING TO THE DELINQUENCY OF A MINOR, MISCHIEF AND CRIMINAL TRESPASS.

...ANOTHER GODDAM COLLISION WITH THE AUTHORITIES...

I NEED TO SMASH SOME WINDOWS ALONG MAIN STREET AND GET OUT OF TOWN AGAIN, TO TRY AND HOOK UP WITH *IZZY* IN LOS ANGELES. I HAD ALREADY HITCHED AND BUSSED UP THERE A COUPLA TIMES...

ALL DAY PAR

HE DID STOOPID THINGS, BUT HE WAS HASSLED BY THE COPS A LOT AND SOMETIMES HE LOOKED LIKE A GIRL -- A LITTLE EFFEMINATE -- AND THEY GAVE HIM HELL FOR THAT. HAVING LONG HAIR WAS NOT COMMON THEM DAYS IN *LAFAYETTE*...

THERE WAS SO LITTLE THERE TO DO... HE'D BE IN FIGHTS A LOT AND I DON'T THINK HE WAS EVEN CONSCIOUS OF WHAT HE DID, OR HOW ANGRY HE GOT.

I ALWAYS THOUGHT THAT THERE WAS SOMETHING CHEMICAL THAT HAPPENED TO HIM WHEN HE WAS ANGRY...

WHEN THEY FOUND OUT IT WAS BILL BAILEY, THEY JUST THREW ME IN THE JAIL.

I KNOW THEY SEE ME AS A *THREAT*. AUTHORITY FIGURES CAN JUST PICK UP MY VIBES TOWARDS THEM AND SEE IT AS A THREAT RIGHT AWAY...

COLUMBIAN PARK AT NIGHT WAS A REALLY COOL PLACE TO BREAK INTO AND HANG OUT ON THE OUTDOOR STAGE AND PLAY THE OLD PIANO THERE FOR HOURS INTO THE NIGHT. MAYBE WE COULD OPEN SOME MINDS IN THE TOWN...

I MOVED TO MY GRANDMA'S PLACE... JUST OVER THE ROAD FROM COLUMBIAN PARK. I HAD MY LITTLE TERRITORIES MARKED OUT LIKE A MUSIC-LOVING ALLEY CAT...

IT WAS 19TH DECEMBER 1982 AND WE QUIT TOWN FOR GOOD THIS TIME... WE HAD THE SAFETY OF GINA'S CAR AND WE DROVE TWO THOUSAND MILES TO LOS ANGELES... NOT LIKE BEFORE WHEN I HAD HITCHHIKED AND GOT THREATENED AND NEARLY RAPED ONE TIME BY SOME GUY... BUT I SAW HIM OFF WITH MY STRAIGHT-EDGED RAZOR...

WE MOVED INTO A DUMP ON 1921 WHITLEY AVENUE IN HOLLYWOOD.

BUS STOP

222

212

Whitley Av.

I HAVE FORMALLY ADOPTED THE NAME W. AXL ROSE AFTER WHAT I DISCOVERED IN MY MOM'S PAPERS IN LAFAYETTE. I DIDN'T WANT TO FULLY SHARE A NAME WITH MY BIOLOGICAL FATHER.

I LIVED ON THE STREETS OFF AND ON FOR FIVE YEARS...

I'D HAVE TO KICK HIM OUT BECAUSE I GOT TIRED OF TRYING TO SUPPORT BOTH OF US AND I GOT TIRED OF ALL THE FIGHTING.

DURING THAT TIME FROM 1982 TO 1985 I LIVED WITH THREE DIFFERENT GUYS. THERE WAS BILL... THERE WAS BILL/AXL... AND THERE WAS AXL... AND ALL THREE WERE A ROYAL PAIN IN THE ASS...

I HOOKED UP WITH IZZY AGAIN, AFTER I GOT ZILCH JOY WHEN I WAS TRYING TO JOIN PUNK BANDS... THEY ALL THOUGHT I SOUNDED TOO MUCH LIKE ROBERT PLANT.

WE ALL HARDLY HAD ENOUGH FOOD TO EAT...

...if you pour yourself out for the hungry and satisfy the desire of the afflicted, then shall your light rise in the darkness and your gloom be as the noonday...

Isaiah 58:10

THE CLUB SCENE IN HOLLYWOOD AND LOS ANGELES WAS HAPPENING MAN...

THERE WERE LOADSA PLACES TO PLAY...

THINGS WERE TAKING SOME SHAPE. I JOINED AN OUTFIT CALLED *RAPIDFIRE* -- I FOUND 'EM IN A LOCAL TRADE PAPER CALLED *RAPID CONNECTION.* WE DID SOME ONE-TAKE-IN-THE-STUDIO DEMOS IN MAY 1983. WE HAWKED THEM AROUND TOWN A BIT, BUT NO ONE WAS BREAKING DOWN OUR DOOR WITH OFFERS OF RICHES, DEALS OR ANYTHING AT ALL...

ME AND IZZY WERE GETTING REAL ANTSY... IT WAS SHIT OR GET OFF THE POT TIME...

ONE CLUB WE HUNG AT IN HOLLYWOOD WAS THE ROXY AND WE CAUGHT A BAND THAT ROCKED BOTH OUR MINDS AND ATTITUDES.

IT WAS GONNA TAKE THREE L-O-O-O-N-G YEARS TO GET A FOOTHOLD IN THE LA MUSIC SCENE... IT FELT LIKE AN ETERNITY... EVEN *LONGER* THAN AN ETERNITY...

ROXY

WE DUG THESE GUYS MOTLEY CRUE.
THEY WERE MAKING A LOT OF NOISE
WITH THEIR ALBUM SHOUT AT THE DEVIL.

VINCE
NEIL AND
TOMMY LEE
ARE WONDERING
JUST WHO THE
FUCK WE
ARE...

IZZY AND ME HOOKED
UP WITH A GUITARIST
CALLED CHRIS WEBER.
WE MET AROUND THE
RAINBOW BAR AND
GRILL ON SUNSET
BOULEVARD.

ANOTHER CAT CALLED
TRACII GUNS CAME OUT
OF FAIRFAX HIGH SCHOOL,
JUST LIKE CHRIS...

WE ALL
STARTED TO HANG
OUT AT PLACES LIKE
THE STARWOOD, THE
WHISKY, MADAME WONG'S,
THE TROUBADOUR...

WELCOME TO THE JUNGLE
ve a Coke
a-Cola
ROOSEVELT
HOTEL
JEWELERS
HOLLYWOOD ROSE
Appearing at The Orphanage
Happy Hour 7-8pm
$1 on entrance
HOLLYWOOD ROSE
Appearing at The Orphanage
Happy Hour 7-8pm
$1 on entrance
HOLLYWOOD ROSE
Appearing at The Orphanage
Happy Hour 7-8pm
$1 on entrance
Happy Hour 7-8pm
$1 on entrance

WE STARTED GIGGING AT THE SMALLER CLUBS AND VENUES... WE PLAYED THE ORPHANAGE, MADAME WONG'S... WE DID THE TROUBADOUR AND THE COUNTRY CLUB...

WE HAD OUR BAND AND AT FIRST I CALLED IT *AXL* AND THEN I CHANGED IT TO *ROSE*... THEN WE BECAME *HOLLYWOOD ROSE*.

ACROSS TOWN SAUL HUDSON WAS GETTING IT TOGETHER WITH A BAND THEY FIRST MONIKERED *TIDUS SLOAN* AND THEN CHANGED TO *ROAD CREW*.

I WAS HALF-HEARTEDLY PLAYING WITH THIS BAND *TIDUS SLOAN*... STEVIE ADLER KEPT SHOWING UP AGAIN AND TELLING ME HE WAS BETTER THAN *OUR* DRUMMER... HE WAS PISSING ME OFF, BUT HE WAS REALLY PERSISTENT, MAN.

WE FORMED A BAND STRAIGHTAWAY... WE CALLED IT ROAD CREW. WE WERE REHEARSING ON SELMA AND HIGHLAND, BUT DUFF AND THE BAND ALL FELL APART IN ABOUT A MONTH. WE WERE SICK OF STEVIE'S PARTYING AND HANGING OUT AND NOT PRACTISING, BUT OUR PATHS WERE GOING TO CROSS AGAIN...

AMONGST ALL THESE CLUSTERS OF LIGHT, THESE SPARKS OF ELECTRICITY... FATE WAS GOING TO PULL US TOGETHER. WE COULD BE THE LUCKY ONES IN A TOWN CHOCK FULL OF HOPEFUL LOSERS... WE COULD TAKE THIS THING ALL THE WAY.

DECEMBER 8TH 1984. NEAR REDONDO BEACH, LOS ANGELES.

MOTLEY CRUE SINGER VINCE NEIL GOT INTO A CAR CRASH AND THE PASSENGER NICK 'RAZZLE' DINGLEY FROM HANOI ROCKS WAS KILLED OUTRIGHT. VINCE DID SOME JAIL TIME AND GOT FINED $2.5 MILLION... IT MADE US FEEL REAL BAD FOR AWHILE...

WE CALLED VICKY HAMILTON, AN AGENT. WE LITERALLY BROUGHT A BOOM BOX ROUND TO THE SILVER LINING ENTERTAINMENT BOOKING AGENCY AND FORCED HER TO LISTEN TO OUR DEMOS. SHE STARTED BOOKING US SHOWS ON THE STRENGTH OF THAT AND OUR IMMEDIATE UPFRONT HUSTLE. WE TOLD HER WE WERE GONNA BE THE BIGGEST BAND IN HOLLYWOOD...

AXL WAS SO FULL OF PENT-UP ENERGY... HE WOULD LITERALLY SHAKE AND TREMBLE WHEN HE GOT UP THERE. IT WAS ALMOST LIKE A CONVULSION, AS IF HE WAS POSSESSED. IT WAS KINDA SCARY SEEING SOMEONE EVOKING ALL THIS POWER, ENERGY AND EMOTION!

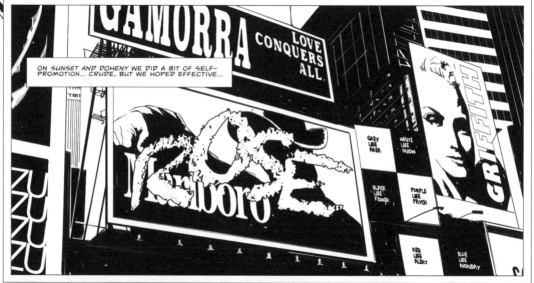

ON SUNSET AND DOHENY WE DID A BIT OF SELF-PROMOTION... CRUDE, BUT WE HOPED EFFECTIVE...

WE WERE ALL CHECKING OUT THE SMALL, INTENSE CIRCLE OF BANDS PLAYING THE CLUB CIRCUIT... WE HEARD THAT CHRIS WEBER HAD BEEN FIRED BY AXL FROM HIS BAND...

HOLLYWOOD ROSE

ME AND STEVE CHECKED OUT THIS GUY W. AXL ROSE WITH THE BAND HOLLYWOOD ROSE AND HE WAS SOMETHING ELSE... BETWEEN THIS OUTFIT AND THE LA GUNS BAND, WE THOUGHT THEY WERE THE BEST TWO IN TOWN.

I GOT TO JOIN HOLLYWOOD ROSE, BUT IZZY STRADLIN TOOK OFF... HE DIDN'T LIKE THE FACT THAT AXL HAD FIRED CHRIS WEBER...

I GOT THE CALL TO GO AUDITION FOR THESE GUYS AFTER CHRIS WEBER WAS CANNED... I ARRIVE AT THIS RAT-INFESTED DUMP ON SELMA AND FRANKLIN... SAME PLACE AS WE HAD USED WITH OUR BAND ROAD CREW.

AXL CAME AND LIVED WITH ME AT MY GRANDMOM'S WITH MY SNAKES AND CATS. HE HUNG OUT WHILE I WAS AT WORK... THEN HE SUDDENLY DISAPPEARED AND CAME BACK TO REHEARSALS AS IF NOTHING HAD HAPPENED.

WE WERE STILL GETTING BOOKINGS AND *HOLLYWOOD ROSE* PLAYED A FEW GIGS INTO 1984... STEVE ADLER AND SLASH WERE IN THE LINEUP ALONG WITH STEVE DARROW AND AXL.

THEN, WOULD YOU BELIEVE IT, HOLLYWOOD ROSE COLLAPSES. BY NOW IZZY IS PLAYING IN A BAND CALLED *LONDON*... AXL GOT HIMSELF HOOKED UP WITH *LA GUNS*... AND I GOT INTO A BAND CALLED *BLACK SHEEP* WITH *WILLIE BASSE*. THAT WAS A GREAT TRAINING GROUND MAN. WILLIE KICKED OFF THE 'SUNSET STRIP ERA', MAN... THREE BANDS, THREE KEGS AND A THOUSAND PEEPS... REALLY GREAT FUN PARTIES AT THE ROXY OR THE WHISKY...

AXL GOT ME A JOB AT *TOWER VIDEO*, JUST ACROSS FROM *TOWER RECORDS*, WHERE I'D GOTTEN BUSTED FOR SHOP-LIFTING ALL THOSE YEARS BACK.

IT WAS GOOD TO SEE AXL AGAIN, BUT HE HAD HOOKED UP WITH MY EX, YVONNE, AND I DIDN'T KNOW HOW I FELT ABOUT THAT.

BOY, WE JUST FUCKED AROUND HUGELY AT TOWER... WE GOT STOCKED UP WITH LIQUOR... PUT PORNO FILMS ON THE IN-STORE VIDEO PLAYERS AND JUST GENERALLY IGNORED ALL THE CUSTOMERS. WE GOT CAUGHT EVENTUALLY, AND GUESS WHO THEY FIRED? RIGHT ON, IT WAS AXL ALRIGHT...

VARIOUS STORIES SWIRL AROUND ABOUT HOW GUNS N' ROSES FINALLY GOT IT TOGETHER AND STARTED THE CLIMB TO THE UPPERMOST REACHES OF ROCK ASCENDANCY.

IT GOES
SOMETHING
LIKE THIS...
OLE BENCH
AND ROB
GARDNER
WERE IN
THE
NASCENT
BAND WITH
AXL AND
TRACII GUNS...

IZZY CAME BACK INTO THE FOLD
AND JOINED AXL, WHO THEN
AMALGAMATED THE NAMES AND
CHOSE GUNS N' ROSES FROM
THE NAMES LA GUNS AND
HOLLYWOOD ROSE.

DUFF CAME IN AND
REPLACED OLE BENCH
ON BASS. THERE WAS
ALSO ANOTHER BAND
AROUND CALLED ROSE...
PLUS YET ANOTHER
PUNK BAND CALLED
ROSE TATTOO.

TRACII HAD A BIG
FALLING OUT WITH
AXL AND BEFORE
TRACII FIRED HIS
ASS, AXL BAILED...

AXL CAME AND ASKED
ME TO START WRITING
WITH IZZY AND SEE
HOW IT SHAPED UP...
EVEN THOUGH IZZY
WAS STILL HEAVILY
INVOLVED WITH THE
PERSIAN BROWN STUFF,
HE WAS STILL HOLDING
HIS OWN. HE WAS THE
GO-TO GUY FOR HIGH
QUALITY PREMIUM
SMACK.

AND ON THE WORLD'S STAGE REAGAN WAS RE-ELECTED WITH A LANDSLIDE MAJORITY... RUSSIA'S GORBACHEV WATCHED THE PROCEEDINGS...

IT WAS THE TIME OF REAGANOMICS... THE TRICKLE DOWN THEORY OF ECONOMIC BULLSHIT...

THE MONEY OF THE SUPER-RICH DOES NOT TRICKLE DOWN TO IMPROVE THE ECONOMY... BUT TENDS TO BE AMASSED AND SHELTERED IN TAX HAVENS WITH A NEGATIVE EFFECT ON THE HOME ECONOMY. RONNIE WAS WELL INSULATED THOUGH...

...THE FUTURE DOESN'T BELONG TO THE FAINTHEARTED; IT BELONGS TO THE BRAVE...

IN MICROCOSMIC TERMS...

...WE NEEDED A BREAK REAL BAD.

WE WENT AHEAD AND DID THE *DUFF*-APPOINTED 'TOUR'. WITH HIS PRIOR CONNECTIONS, *DUFF* HAD MANAGED TO STRING A FEW DATES TOGETHER FOR US. ON THE WAY, THE FIRST VAN DIED IN BAKERSFIELD, SO WE LEFT OUR ROAD CREW, DANNY AND JOE, WITH OUR MUSICAL GEAR AND SOLDIERED ON... OUR DRIVER WAS REALLY GNARLY, MAN... HE WAS EATING SPEED TO STAY AWAKE AND WAS GETTING MORE AND MORE FRIED BY THE MINUTE...

WE NEED TO BAIL OUT FROM THIS AND MAKE IT TO SEATTLE WITHOUT THIS GUY AT THE WHEEL...

WE HITCHED UP TO SEATTLE TO TRY AND MAKE THAT FINAL LEG OF THE 'TOUR'... THE LAST GIG... BUT SOMEHOW WE DIDN'T GET OUR GEAR.

5 NORTH
Seattle

DONNER, DUFF'S FRIEND IN SEATTLE, WAS EXPECTING US FIVE DUDES TO SHOW AND WE DULY OBLIGED. WE GOT THERE AND IT WAS A SCENE SURROUNDED BY POT AND BOOZE, WITH PLENTY OF STONERS EVERYWHERE...

WE PLAYED GORILLA GARDENS, A SMALL ROOM NEAR FREMONT SEATTLE. IT WAS A RANK DUMP THAT WOULD HAVE GIVEN ANY SELF-RESPECTING RODENT THE SHITS.

IT WAS THAT NIGHT PLAYING IN THAT HOLE THAT CEMENTED WHAT WAS TO BE THE GUNS N' ROSES LINEUP... THAT TRIP AND THE ADVERSITY REALLY BONDED US.

GORILLA GARDENS

DUFF'S OLD BAND THE FASTBACKS SUPPORTED AND PEOPLE WERE REAL HAPPY TO SEE DUFF BACK IN TOWN.

GUNS and ROSES
Featuring
ex-Ten Minute Warning
member Duff McKagan
WITH
FASTBACKS
plus 5150
SAT., JUNE 8
ROCK THEATER

WE SPENT SOME TIME BEGGING FOR CHANGE IN SEATTLE BEFORE WE HIGHTAILED IT OUT OF THERE. WE WENT BACK VIA SACRAMENTO WITH A FRIEND, JILL, WHO WAS GREG'S GIRLFRIEND, AND WE DROVE ALL THE WAY TO LA WITHOUT STOPPING.

WE GOT BROADSIDED BY SOME ASSHOLE DRIVING AT SIXTY MILES AN HOUR AS WE PULLED OUT AT AN INTERSECTION. STEVIE GOT A REAL BUSTED UP ANKLE... EVERYONE GOT BANGED UP EXCEPT SLASH.

WE WERE STOKED, MAN. WE GOT OUR GEAR BACK, ALTHOUGH WE MISSED A COUPLA GIGS, BUT WE HAD MADE IT TO SEATTLE IN ONE PIECE AND THEN GOT BACK TO HOME BASE. THAT WAS OUR ACID TEST, IF YOU WILL... THE CEMENT THAT MADE THE BAND CONTINUE. BREAK THE MOULD TO MAKE THE MOULD...

AS THE BAND WAS GETTING IT TOGETHER IT ALMOST DIED TOGETHER... AND NOBODY WOULDA CARED OR EVEN KNOWN...

GALLY'S

AFTER ALL THAT WE GOT A REHEARSAL PLACE IN SANTA MONICA, RIGHT BY GARDNER STREET. 1139 NORTH FULLER AVENUE TO BE EXACT. TWO DUDES, WEST ARKEEN AND DEL JAMES, HIRED IT OUT TO US... NOT THAT THE RENT EVER GOT PAID. WE DUBBED IT THE HELLHOUSE. IT WAS REAL GNARLY... IT STUCK OUT LIKE THE HOUSE FROM THAT FILM PSYCHO.

WE COULDN'T BELIEVE SOME OF THESE ASSHOLES FROM THE MAJOR LABELS. THEY WERE WINING AND DINING US, WHICH WAS A REALLY GREAT WAY TO STAY ALIVE. THEN ONE FUCKER FROM CHRYSALIS OFFERED US $750,000 AND THEY HADN'T EVEN HEARD US. WE WERE LIKE, JUST GO FUCK YOURSELF! AT FIRST...

WORD OF MOUTH WAS GROWING... WE KICKED ASS ONSTAGE... WE DIDN'T POSE... WE WERE THE REAL DEAL. AUDIENCES HAD GROWN TO AROUND 700 BY THAT TIME IN THE CLUBS...

ALL THE LOSERS FROM ALL THE OTHER BANDS AROUND SUNSET BOULEVARD CAME TO THE HANGOUT... WE CRANKED UP THOSE TWO MARSHALL AMPLIFIERS AND COULD BE HEARD AT LEAST TEN FUCKIN' BLOCKS AWAY.

IT COULDA LOOKED LIKE WE WERE LOSING IT, BUT WHILE ALL THIS CRAZY MADNESS WAS GOING ON AROUND US WE WERE ZEROING IN ON CHRYSALIS AND GEFFEN. THEY WERE TALKING BIG MONEY AND OPENING UP THEIR CHEQUE BOOKS...

AXL WAS KEEPING A VERY COOL HEAD AND STAYING CALM WHILST THE BIDDING WAR WENT ON AROUND US. TOM ZUTAUT FROM GEFFEN WAS EDGING CLOSER AND CLOSER TO AXL...

THIS GUY DON'T SEEM THAT SAVVY... MORE LIKE AN ANIMAL OUTTA THE AFRICAN JUNGLE. BUT I'M GONNA OFFER THEM A CONTRACT WITH GEFFEN.

JUNKYARD

TOM, I MADE A MISTAKE DUDE... I TOLD THE CHRYSALIS A&R WOMAN THAT IF SHE WALKED NAKED FROM THEIR OFFICE DOWN SUNSET BOULEVARD TO TOWER RECORDS WE WOULD SIGN WITH THEM.

AXL, WHAT THE FUCK MAN? I'M GONNA LOSE THE DEAL BECAUSE OF THIS? AXL, WE'RE IN THE MIDDLE OF MAKING A DEAL HERE! YOU CAN'T DO THIS!

INSIDE LOT 619 WE PARTIED AND PLAYED INTO THE WEE SMALL HOURS... ATTRACTING A CROSS-SECTION OF GENERALISED WEIRDOS, FOXY VIXENS AND WANNABE ROCKERS.

IT WASN'T ALL GOOD AS SOMETIMES AMBULANCES HAD TO BE CALLED FOR O.D.'S ON OUR PATCH... SOME OF THE HANGERS-ON DIDN'T HANG SO TOUGH...

MARCH 25TH 1986. GEFFEN RECORDS, SUNSET BOULEVARD.

WE SIGNED OUR MAJOR RECORDING CONTRACT WITH GEFFEN.

'OUR' GIRLS WERE DANCING
AT THE SEVENTH VEIL STRIP
CLUB ON SUNSET, THEY WERE
HANGING OUT AT OUR PLACE...
AND THEY WERE DANCING
ONSTAGE AT OUR SHOWS...

QUAALUDES, DOPE, COKE,
SPEED, VALIUM AND BOOZE
WERE ALL AROUND, JUST
EVERYWHERE...

Seventh Veil

GIRLS
GIRLS
GIRLS

MAKE
YOURSELF
RIGHT AT
HOME
GIRLS
GIRLS
GIRLS

ATM
MOTEL
HOTEL

YOU WOULD ALSO FIND US, IF YOU COULD
SEE US IN THE MURK, HANGING OUT AT
EL COMPADRE CANTINA ON SUNSET...
WE LIKED TO KEEP IT LOCAL.

WE STILL
FREQUENTED ALL
THE USUAL DIVES...
EL COMPADRE ON SUNSET
WAS ANOTHER FAVOURITE
HANG. I DID SOME DEALS
THERE AND I COULD GET
REAL MELLOWED OUT
AWAY FROM THE
CRAZINESS OF THE
HELLHOUSE...

IZZY WAS STAYING WITH HIS
FRIENDS AT FLOOR LEVEL,
HANGING OUT WITH THE
ROACHES IN THE HELLHOUSE.
HE WOULD BE PASSED OUT
AND STRUNG OUT FOR THREE
DAYS IN A ROW SOMETIMES.

PEOPLE WERE STARTING TO TALK ABOUT OUR CRAZED LIFESTYLE. THE HOUSE ON NORTH FULLER WAS BEGINNING TO ATTRACT TOO MUCH ATTENTION... WE SOMETIMES HAD 500 KIDS HANGING OUT THERE PARTYING. WE SOLD 'EM BEER AT A BUCK A BOTTLE OUTTA THE BACK OF THE VAN.

MEANWHILE, THROUGHOUT ALL THIS, WE KEPT REHEARSING AND EVEN GOT DOWN ON SOME SERIOUSLY SWEATY FUNK. WE REALLY DUG 'WORD UP' BY CAMEO...

PRETTY LADIES AROUND THE WORLD...

AXL WAS FIXATED ON VIDEO SHLOCK HORRORS AND NASTY PORN, AND HE ALSO JUST LOVED WATCHING SID VICIOUS ON MTV... HE WATCHED IT AGAIN AND AGAIN...

MAN, I SURE WOULD LOVE TO HAVE THE SEX PISTOLS PRODUCER BILL PRICE WORK ON OUR SOUND, LIKE REAL AGGRESSIVE...

WE WAITED FOR THE RECORD DEAL ADVANCE TO ARRIVE. WE ALSO HAD TO AVOID OUR DOPE DEALERS, AS WE OWED THEM MONEY AND WANTED TO KEEP OUR FINGERS AND HANDS AND ARMS AND LEGS, TOO. WE NEEDED 'EM FOR OUR DAY JOB...

THE LAWYERS HAD TO TAKE CARE OF LOADS OF HASSLE... AXL'S POLICE RECORD... SLASH DIDN'T WANT DAVID GEFFEN TO KNOW WHO HIS FATHER WAS... THERE WAS ALSO A PROBLEM WITH AXL'S NAME... LIKE, WHAT WAS IT FOR REAL? AND THEY MISSPELLED SLASH'S NAME, APTLY, AS 'STASH' ON THE CONTRACT AT FIRST...

NOW WE COULD AFFORD BREAKFAST AT HAMBURGER HAMLET EVERY DAY.

MARCH 28TH 1986 AND WE WERE WINNING. OUR TWO HOUSE SHOWS AT THE ROXY WERE A SELLOUT.

DANCE YOR ASS OFF/DRINK YOUR FACE OFF/GET YOUR ROCKS OFF/ GUNS N' ROSES 2 SHOWS/8 & 10PM/ROXY THEATER

WELCOME TO THE ROXY. IS EVERYONE NICE AND RELAXED? THANKS FOR COMING OUT...

BUT IT'S THE POLICE, GUYS... THIS SONG IS CALLED 'THEY'RE OUT TO GET ME'!!!

WE ARE KILLING ONSTAGE... WELCOME TO OUR JUNGLE...

...WE GOT FUN AND GAMES...

I MEAN WE WERE KILLING IT...

...IF YOU GOT THE MONEY, HONEY... WE GOT YOUR DISEASE

THESE BLACKOUTS ONSTAGE WERE VERY COOL... AS WE NEEDED TO SNORT SOME BLOW OFFA THE AMPS AND MONITORS...

MY STEPDAD, STEPHEN BAILEY, IS COMING TO TOWN FROM INDIANA TO SEE ME. WONDER WHAT HIS ANGLE IS... WHAT DOES HE WANT AFTER ALL THIS TIME? PROBABLY GOING TO TRY AND MANAGE ME AND TRY TO DO SOME SHYSTER ROOK...

HOLLYWOOD'S ARNIE STIEFEL WAS AN OLD TIME HOLLYWOOD IMPRESARIO... HE MANAGED SINGER *ROD STEWART,* AMONG OTHERS. HE WAS INTERESTED IN MANAGING THE BAND AND AS A GESTURE OF GOODWILL HE LOANED US A RENTED HOUSE... *BAD MOVE ARNOLD!*

THEY WOULD GO ON DRUG-CRAZED RAMPAGES AND REALLY GO BERSERK... IT WAS TOTALLY DISGUSTING. THE PLACE WAS FULL OF SHIT, LITERALLY, WHERE THEY JUST DUMPED EVERYWHERE...

STIEFEL WALKED AWAY IN DISGUST WITH A REPAIR BILL FOR $22,000.

VICKY HAMILTON WAS BOOKING THE GIGS BUT WE NEEDED SOME STRONG MANAGEMENT. OUR BEHAVIOUR WAS SO NUTS THAT IT WAS TURNING OUT TO BE PROBLEMATIC. WE MOVED TO A NEW PAD ON FOUNTAIN AVENUE IN WEST HOLLYWOOD BUT OUR CRAZED ALL-NIGHT PARTIES SOON DROVE DOWN THE PROPERTY VALUES AROUND THERE.

POOR VICKY, WE BUSTED THAT WOMAN'S ASS TWENTY-FOUR HOURS A DAY... SHE WAS ULTRA IMPORTANT IN THOSE EARLY DAYS. HER SUPPORT...THE BOOKINGS... THE CASH INPUT... EVERYTHING REALLY...

TIM COLLINS TRIED TO MASSAGE A MANAGEMENT SITUATION WITH GUNS N' ROSES BUT IT BECAME EVIDENT THAT THINGS WERE WAY OUT OF HIS ORBIT. WE WOULD CROSS PATHS WITH HIM AND AEROSMITH A LITTLE FURTHER DOWN THE LINE THOUGH...

TIM COLLINS, WHO MANAGED AEROSMITH, WAS COMING STRONGLY INTO FOCUS TO MANAGE US... WITH PRESSURE FROM TOM ZUTAUT AND MORE SO FROM DAVID GEFFEN, WHO WAS AS ADMIRED AS HE WAS FEARED IN THE INDUSTRY. TIM WAS TRYING TO REVERSE THE COLLATERAL DAMAGE TO AEROSMITH, WITH ALL THEIR ADDICTION PROBLEMS AND THE RESULTANT DOWNWARD CAREER TRAJECTORY.

JOE PERRY, AEROSMITH'S GUITAR MAVEN, DIDN'T WANT ME MANAGING THESE GUYS AS HE HAD BEEN COPPING DOPE FROM THEM BEFORE... I WAS ON A MESSIANIC MISSION TO CLEAN AEROSMITH RIGHT THE WAY UP. THE DRUGS AND BOOZE HAD RADDLED THE BAND TOTALLY.

HEY JOE, MAN, I AM OUTTA HERE. I INVITED THEM BACK TO THE LE DUFY HOTEL TO PARLAY AND ONE OF THEM WAS LOCKED IN THE BATHROOM FOR OVER FOUR HOURS. I CAN'T DEAL WITH THESE DERANGERS. THIS IS TOTAL AND ABSOLUTE SKEEZE... MINE, YOURS AND OUR COLLECTIVE SOBRIETY IS AT STAKE HERE. THEY ALSO RAN UP A BAR BILL OF OVER FOUR HUNDRED AND FIFTY BUCKS WHILE I WAS SLEEPING...

POTENTIAL MANAGERS AND PRODUCERS ALSO INCLUDED KIM FOWLEY, WHO THEN - WHEN WE REJECTED HIS ADVANCES - WANTED TO BUY OUR SONG 'WELCOME TO THE JUNGLE' FOR $10,000. WE NIXED THAT TOO. MOTLEY CRUE'S PRODUCER TOM WERMAN ALSO HEARD US, HATED US AND LEFT...

Denny's

$10,000.00

AS A PRECURSOR TO OUR IMPENDING ALBUM, GEFFEN PUT OUT AN EP CALLED LIVE?!* @ LIKE A SUICIDE. IT WAS A SORTA INDIE RELEASE AND A SORTA HOLDING DEVICE FOR THE FANS AS THE ALBUM PROPER WAS STILL A WAYS OFF...

WE RELEASED IT ON THE UZI SUICIDE LABEL, WHICH WAS REALLY JUST A GEFFEN SUB-LABEL... TWO ORIGINALS AND TWO COVER VERSIONS. 'RECKLESS LIFE', 'MOVE TO THE CITY' BY US AND 'NICE BOYS' AND 'MAMA KIN' BY ROSE TATTOO AND AEROSMITH RESPECTIVELY. WE MADE SURE THE INTRO WOULD WAKE YOU UP, TOO...

THE EP'S A PIECE OF SHIT COMPARED TO THE UPCOMING ALBUM... THAT'S THE MOST CONTRIVED BIT OF SHIT WE'VE DONE YET. IT AIN'T A LIVE RECORD. IF YOU THINK IT IS YOU'RE CRAZY. WHAT WE DID WAS GO INTO A ROOM AND RECORD OURSELVES AND THEN ADD 50,000 SCREAMING PEOPLE ON TOP.

HEY FUCKERS SUCK ON GUNS AND FUCKING ROSES!

THE HANGERS-ON AROUND US CHANGED EVERY DAY... AND SO DID THE DRUGS. CRACK COCAINE ENTERED ALL OF OUR LANDSCAPES...

WOW MAN! THIS IS SOMETHING ELSE... I FEEL LIKE A GOD. I CAN DO ANYTHING. HIT ME AGAIN, DUDE... THIS IS TOOOOOO MUCH!

AXL ROSE WAS AVOIDING THE COPS AROUND THEN. HE WAS WANTED FOR QUESTIONING ON A SOUPED-UP ALLEGED RAPE CHARGE. EVENTUALLY THE CHARGES GOT DROPPED, BUT THE 'INCIDENT' INSPIRED A GREAT SONG: 'OUT TO GET ME'.

THIS CHARGE IS BOGUS, BUT I AM GONNA LIE LOW UNTIL THE CHARGES ARE DROPPED. THE COPS ARE ALWAYS AFTER ME...

WALK

IVAR A

←1500 N.

WE HAD OPENED FOR MR ALICE COOPER IN SANTA BARBARA AND OUR GIG SCHEDULE WAS RAMPING UP... FAST. AXL WAS NOT ALLOWED INTO THE VENUE THAT NIGHT AS HIS NAME WAS NOT ON THE GIG LIST, SO WE HAD TO PERFORM WITHOUT HIM.

ALICE COOPER WAS PISSING EVERYONE OFF WITH HIS ONSTAGE ANTICS. HE HAD HIS GREAT ALBUM CONSTRICTOR RELEASED AROUND THEN... AND THE FURORE HE HAD CAUSED WHEN HE HAD STARTED OUT WAS STILL STICKING TO HIM.

THE ADVANCE MONEY WAS GREAT BUT WE WERE SPENDING IT FAST. AXL SOMETIMES KEPT HIS MONEY HIDDEN UNDER THE SOFA AT VICKY HAMILTON'S PAD IN A ROLLED UP SOCK. WE GOT ALL THE SONGWRITING ROYALTY WRANGLES SORTED OUT AND DIVIDED THE DOUGH EQUAL WAYS THROUGHOUT THE BAND.

I'VE GOT $7,500 SECRETED IN MY NEW COWBOY BOOTS...

OCTOBER 31ST 1986. WE OPENED FOR THE RED HOT CHILI PEPPERS... ALSO HENRY ROLLINS FROM BLACK FLAG GAVE US HIS BLESSING, GAVE US THE THUMBS UP. THESE GUYS HAD BEEN TOGETHER FOR A DECADE AND THEY HAD THE UTMOST CREDIBILITY.

THESE GUY ARE KICKASS... THEY ARE FOR REAL... THEY ARE BLOWING EVERYONE ELSE OFF THE STAGE...

THE SEARCH FOR A PRODUCER WHO DIDN'T WANT A MILLION DOLLARS UPFRONT TO WALK IN THE STUDIO AND TAKE A CUT OF OUR FUTURE ROYALTIES WAS STILL ON... FINALLY, MIKE CLINK, WHO HAD WORKED WITH *TRIUMPH* (A BAND WE DIDN'T REALLY LIKE), SAID HE WAS RADICALLY RARING TO WORK WITH US.

MIKE CLINK WANTED TO RECORD US LIVE AND HOT. NO MESSING AND NO STUDIO TRICKERY... JUST BALLS-TO-THE-WALL ROCK 'N' ROLL. WE HAD WRITTEN MOST OF THE TWELVE SONGS ALREADY WHILE GIGGING, HANGING OUT AND REHEARSING... PRETTY GOOD FOR FIVE DEGENERATE SCUMBAGS.

WE WANTED TO REWIRE THE ROCK WORLD WITH THIS RECORD. THE EIGHTIES WERE ALL ABOUT A POLISHED SOUND... FUCK ALL THE AIRBRUSHING... WE WANNA SET THE RECORD STRAIGHT.

THE ROCK WORLD HAS SUCKED A BIG FUCKING DICK SINCE THE SEX PISTOLS COLLAPSED AND WE ARE HERE TO REDRESS THE BALANCE. WE AIN'T PRETENDERS, WE ARE THE REAL DEAL...

WE CHECKED OUT THE LONDON UNDERGROUND...
A TRIP TO SEE *THE REPLACEMENTS* WAS IN ORDER,
BUT WE ENDED UP GETTING TOTALLY LOST AND
TOTALLY FUCKED UP.

CAN'T WAIT
TO HIT THOSE *LONDON*
AUDIENCES WITH SOME
TOTAL ABANDON... AFTER A
YEAR OF HARDLY PLAYING,
WE WANT TO HIT THE
STAGE RUNNING.

WE GOT OUR MANAGER FINALLY,
A GUY CALLED ALAN NIVEN. HE
TRIED TO IMPOSE SOME ORDER
ON OUR STREET LEVEL CHAOS.
THERE WAS TO BE NO DRUGS IN
THE STUDIO... JACK DANIELS AND
CIGARETTES WERE OK, BUT THAT
WAS IT!

GEFFEN RECORDS HAD ALLOCATED A RECORDING BUDGET
ADVANCE OF $375,000 AND WERE GETTING ANTSY. SLASH
TURNED BLUE AT ONE STAGE DURING THE RECORDINGS...
THEY WERE THREATENING TO NOT PAY THE SECOND PART
OF THE ADVANCE UNLESS THE BAND STARTED TO CLEAN
UP THEIR ACT.

I WAS JUST
ABOUT ONLY TALKING
TO IZZY AS WE WERE
THE TWO STONE COLD JUNKIES
IN THE BAND. SOMETIMES I
CAN'T STAND UP FOR FALLING
DOWN... LOS ANGELES WAS
TOTALLY AWASH WITH
HEROIN BY THEN...

WE RECORDED
APPETITE FOR DESTRUCTION
AND I TOLD 'EM NO DRUGS IN
THE STUDIO AT ALL. WE STARTED
RECORDING AT TAKE ONE STUDIO AND
THEN AROUND JANUARY 1987 WE MOVED
TO RUMBO RECORDERS OUT IN
CANOGA PARK, SAN FERNANDO VALLEY.
AXL DROVE EVERYONE NUTS
AS HE PATCHED HIS VOCALS
IN LINE BY LINE ON
EACH SONG.

NIVEN WAS FROM
A SET UP CALLED
STRAVINSKY BROS.
MANAGEMENT AND
WE DON'T THINK HE
THOUGHT WE WERE
GONNA REALLY
HAPPEN... MAYBE
WE'D SELL AROUND
20,000 COPIES
OF THE RECORD
OR SOMETHING...

ALL THE LA BANDS WANTED TO STEEP THEMSELVES IN THE HEROIN CHIC...
G N' R GAVE THE DRUG AN ADDED MYSTIQUE AND CONFERRED ON THE DEADLY
POWDERED DRUG THE SEEMINGLY ADDED POTENTIAL TO ACHIEVE ROCK 'N' ROLL
SUCCESS...

SMACK EQUALLED THE GIDDY HEIGHTS
OF ROCK STARDOM, BUT THE REALITY
WAS FAR MORE SQUALID AND SEAMY.

COME TO TAKE AWAY OUR YOUNG ONES...
SOMETIMES QUICKLY, SOMETIMES SLOWLY...
OUR YOUNG TALENT BROUGHT AWAY IN YOUR
COLD, EMOTIONLESS EMBRACE...

TODD CREW, OUR BASSIST FRIEND FROM JETBOY,
HAD JUST OD'D ON HEROIN. HE HAD GOTTEN REALLY
FUCKED UP AND HERE WAS THE UTTERLY HORRIBLE
REALITY... THE SQUALID CONSEQUENCES. TODD WAS
GONE, GONE FOREVER...

WE HAD FLOWN
TO NEW YORK TO
PLAY THE NEW MUSIC
SEMINAR, MAN. TODD DYING WAS
JUST HORRIBLY UNBEARABLE...
IT WAS TOO MUCH TO TAKE IN.
HIS MOM HAD CALLED AFTER THE
NEW YORK POLICE DEPARTMENT
HAD TOLD HER THEY HAD HIS DEAD
BODY. I WAS NUMB, BUT IT STILL
HIT THROUGH TO ME... HE WAS
FOUND IN SLASH'S HOTEL ROOM
AT THE MILFORD PLAZA. HE DIED
IN SLASH'S ARMS AT JUST
TWENTY-ONE YEARS
OF AGE...

TODD CREW

SEPTEMBER 2, 1965
JULY 18, 1987

BELOVED SON

BAD BLOOD SEEPED OUT
ONTO THE HOLLYWOOD
STRIP AS THE MEMBERS OF
JETBOY CLAIMED SLASH WAS
RESPONSIBLE FOR TODD'S
DEMISE...

I REGRET
NOT TALKING TO TODD
BEFORE HE WENT TO NEW YORK.
I'D FELT A MASSIVE NEED TO TALK
TO HIM OUT OF MY CONCERN FOR
HIS WELL BEING, BUT I WAS NOT AWARE
ENOUGH TO REALISE THAT I DIDN'T
HAVE THE TIME THAT I THOUGHT
I DID. I THOUGHT I'D
HAVE TIME
LATER...

JULY 21ST 1987. IT WAS FINALLY RELEASED... OUR SELF-DESCRIPTIVE DEBUT APPETITE FOR DESTRUCTION. A CAMPAIGN SWUNG INTO PLACE AND THEN...

NOTHING.

ROBERT WILLIAMS' ORIGINAL COVER ART WAS PLACED INSIDE A SECOND ALBUM COVER, AS THE FIRST ONE WAS DEEMED TOO CONTROVERSIAL AND SEVERAL RETAILERS REFUSED TO STOCK IT... EVEN IF IT WAS BROWN BAGGED TO COVER THE ARTWORK.

WE HAD MANAGED TO BOTTLE THE BAND'S INTENSITY ON THE RECORDING... IT WAS TOUGH, ROUGH AND MEAN.

WE BEGAN TO GIG AGAIN IN EARNEST. WE DID A STRING OF DATES WITH THE CULT AND THEIR LEAD SINGER IAN ASTBURY SEEMED TO BE IN OUR DRESSING ROOM ALLA THE TIME.

WE WERE OWNING THOSE SHOWS AND IN ATLANTA, GEORGIA, THERE WAS A NEAR RIOT AS AXL HAD REPORTEDLY PUNCHED A SECURITY GUY BEFORE THE SHOW. THE POLICE STORMED THE STAGE AND IT WAS ALL ADDING TO OUR CREDIBILITY WITH THE FANS.

WE GOT ON TO RECORDING A VIDEO FOR 'WELCOME TO THE JUNGLE'. WE SHOT IT AT PARK PLAZA AND 450 SOUTH LA BREA IN HOLLYWOOD... IT WAS ALL 'HURRY UP AND WAIT' AND WE WERE NOT USED TO THE STOP-START THING WITH FILMING. WE PLAYED IT SIX OR SEVEN TIMES BEFORE WE NAILED IT AND THEN WE DID A SET FOR THE AUDIENCE...

EXIT

SLASH WAS COMING OFF THE SMACK... THE TODD CREW THING HAD SHOCKED HIM TO THE CORE. HE SHOWED THE CLASSIC ADDICT BEHAVIOUR OF SWOPPING ONE ADDICTION FOR ANOTHER AND STARTED SWIMMING IN A SEA OF JACK AND OTHER BOOZE...

DRINK BECAME A SUBSTITUTE AND I KINDA FORGOT ABOUT SMACK. THANK GOD I WAS WEARING LEATHER PANTS, THEY WERE MORE FORGIVING... AS I WAS GETTING INTO THE THING OF PISSING MYSELF PLENTY, A LOT OF THE TIME...

GROUPIES WERE EVERYWHERE ON THE TOUR. THEY WERE OUT IN FULL FORCE IN ARIZONA... THEY WERE EQUAL OPPORTUNITY, ANY-BAND-ANY-TIME TYPES OF GROUPIES. THEY WERE DOWN TO FUCK ANYONE AND AT ALL TIMES.

WE WERE GIGGING ALL YEAR... 1987 WAS A FULL ON GIGGING SCHEDULE AND WE WERE OPENING FOR THE CULT.

SEPTEMBER 4TH 1987. WE WERE A FORCE TO BE RECKONED WITH AT THE SDSU OPEN AIR THEATRE IN SAN DIEGO. AXL OFFERED THE AUDIENCE SOME SAGE ADVICE...

I GOT A TIP. IF YOU AIN'T GOT NO MONEY, AND YOU WANNA GET FUCKED UP, YOU FIND THESE LIQUOR STORES THAT THE WINOS HIT UP, YOU KNOW. AND RIGHT BESIDE THUNDERBIRD, YOU'LL FIND A BOTTLE OF NIGHT TRAIN... THAT'LL FUCK YOU UP TWICE AS BAD AS THUNDERBIRD AND IT'S ONLY A BUCK AND A QUARTER. IF YOU DRINK A QUART, I DON'T CARE HOW BAD YOU ARE, YOU'RE GONNA BLACK OUT. THIS SONG IS CALLED 'NIGHT TRAIN'...

AXL CERTAINLY WAS NOT DIALLING DOWN ANY OF HIS ONSTAGE INVECTIVES.

HE DIDN'T SEEM TO CARE WHO OR WHAT HE OFFENDED.

WE'RE GONNA DO A TUNE CALLED 'MOVE TO THE CITY'... Y'KNOW, BEFORE WE DO THE SONG, I WANNA SAY HOW SOME OF THE OLDER GENERATION ROCK STARS GOT A LOT OF SHIT TO SAY ABOUT G N' R... BUT HEAR THIS, G N' R AREN'T TRYING TO BE NOBODY BUT THEMSELVES AND PEOPLE LIKE PAUL STANLEY FROM KISS CAN SUCK MY DICK... AND SOME OF THESE OLD GUYS THAT SAY WE'RE RIPPING THEM OFF, MAYBE THEY SHOULD LISTEN TO SOME OF THEIR EARLIER ALBUMS AND REMEMBER HOW TO PLAY THEM...

STEVE ADLER AND HIS HEROIN USE WAS STILL AN ONGOING PROBLEM. STEVE WAS FLAKING. HE WENT AND PUNCHED A WALL AND INJURED HIS HAND BEFORE ONE SHOW IN MICHIGAN AND WE HAD TO DRAFT IN DRUMMER FRED COURY FROM CINDERELLA TO TEMPORARILY REPLACE HIM.

FRED PLAYED TECHNICALLY GOOD AND STEADY, BUT THE SONGS SOUNDED JUST AWFUL. THEY WERE WRITTEN WITH STEVE PLAYING THE DRUMS AND HIS SENSE OF SWING WAS THE PUSH AND PULL THAT GAVE THE SONGS THEIR FEEL. I WOULD HAVE PREFERRED TO CONTINUE WITH STEVE, BUT WE COULDN'T WAIT ANY LONGER. HE WASN'T READY TO CLEAN UP.

ON 23RD DECEMBER AT THE FRANKLIN PLAZA HOTEL OUR FRIEND NIKKI SIXX FROM MOTLEY CRUE HAD A NEAR CATASTROPHIC BRUSH WITH DISASTER. EARLIER THAT NIGHT SIXX HAD ARRIVED AT SLASH'S HOTEL SCORING SOME BAGS OF SMACK ON THE WAY...

AT THE HOTEL, THE DEALER TIED NIKKI OFF AND HIT HIM WITH SOME "SWEET" PERSIAN BROWN HEROIN. AS HE FELL OUT OF HIS CHAIR AND TURNED BLUE, STEVE ADLER DRAGGED HIM INTO THE SHOWER AND BLASTED HIM WITH COLD WATER. THE NEWS LEAKED OUT THAT SIXX WAS DEAD... ANOTHER FATAL AND TRAGIC ROLL OF THE DICE...

NIKKI HAD OTHER IDEAS... HE WAS IN A FORM OF RUDE HEALTH... ROCK 'N' ROLL MADNESS WAS AT ITS ZENITH. AS HE LAY CONNECTED TO TUBES IN THE HOSPITAL NIKKI WAS BEING QUESTIONED BY A COP. HE TOLD THE COP TO GET FUCKED AND STAGGERED OUT OF THE HOSPITAL, SURPRISING TWO FANS WHO THOUGHT HE WAS DEAD. THEY GAVE HIM A LIFT BACK HOME...

I FEEL LIKE MY SKIN IS ROTTING OFF ME... I SMELL LIKE SHIT AND MY SHIT HAS MORE AND MORE TRACES OF BLOOD IN IT. I FEEL LIKE I'M ABOUT TO BURST INTO TEARS AT ANY MINUTE... I HAVE A PILE OF CLOTHES IN THE CLOSET WITH SHIT ALL OVER THEM. HOW ABOUT THIS? I CALLED THE HOTEL FRONT DESK LAST NIGHT IN TOKYO AND COMPLAINED ABOUT OUR FANS BANGING ON MY WINDOW. FUCK! I'M ON THE 26TH FLOOR!

MY NAME IS DOC MCGHEE... I WAS ALWAYS GETTING FRENZIED EARLY HOURS PHONE CALLS.

NIKKI WAS ALWAYS SEEING MEXICANS AND MIDGETS RUNNING AROUND HIS HOUSE... OR THE LA POLICE DEPARTMENT WOULD CALL ME BECAUSE HIS NEIGHBOUR HAD PHONED THEM TO REPORT THAT HE WAS CRAWLING AROUND HIS GARDEN IN THE MIDDLE OF THE NIGHT WITH A SHOTGUN. THIS SHIT WAS GOING ON TWICE EVERY WEEK...

SLASH WAS PRETTY RATTLED BUT NOT TOTALLY CONVERTED BY NIKKI'S NEAR-DEATH EXPERIENCE. THINGS WITH HIM CONTINUED IN THE SAME VEIN... PARDON THE PUN...

WE PLAYED OUT THE YEAR WITH FOUR GREAT SHOWS AT PERKINS PALACE IN PASADENA... EVEN THOUGH STEVE WAS SIDELINED WITH HIS BUSTED HAND.

WE STARTED 1988 WITH AXL LEAVING THE BAND...

HE JUST WALKED OUT.

THREE DAYS LATER HE WAS BACK...

AND WE SHOT ANOTHER VIDEO FOR 'SWEET CHILD O' MINE' IN HUNTINGTON, CALIFORNIA.

ALL THROUGH JANUARY TO JUNE WE OPENED SHOWS FOR IRON MAIDEN. WE HATED EACH OTHER BIG TIME. WE WEREN'T EVEN ON SPEAKING TERMS BY THE END OF THAT TOUR.

THE REST OF THE YEAR WAS SPENT OPENING FOR AEROSMITH ON THEIR PERMANENT VACATION TOUR. WE BLEW RIGHT UP DURING THAT TOUR AND ON AUGUST 6TH, APPETITE FOR DESTRUCTION WENT TO NUMBER ONE FOR THREE WEEKS, ALMOST A YEAR AFTER WE RELEASED IT.

BY THE END OF THE TOUR, GUNS N' ROSES WERE HUGE... THEY BASICALLY JUST EXPLODED. WE WERE ALL PISSED THAT ROLLING STONE SHOWED UP TO DO A STORY ON MY BAND AEROSMITH, BUT GUNS N' ROSES ENDED UP ON THE COVER OF THE MAGAZINE... SUDDENLY, THE OPENING ACT WAS BIGGER THAN WE WERE. BUT WE FELT SORRY FOR THEM. ONE, THEY WERE SO FUCKED UP IT WAS RIDICULOUS. TWO, THEIR STUPID MANAGER HAD NEGOTIATED A BAD DEAL FOR THEM AND NEVER BOTHERED TO RENEGOTIATE IT OR EVEN COMPLAIN. THREE, THEY WERE TRAVELLING LIKE GYPSIES, THEIR OLD SUITCASES HELD TOGETHER BY TWINE AND GAFFER TAPE. AT THE END OF THE TOUR, WE BOUGHT THEM ALL NEW HALLIBURTON CASES, WHICH THEIR MANAGER TOOK AS AN INSULT.

BY SEPTEMBER 10TH WE HAD THE BILLBOARD NUMBER ONE SINGLE WITH 'SWEET CHILD O' MINE'.

I THOUGHT THE RIFF WAS REALLY SILLY AND I HATED PLAYING IT, BUT IT TURNS OUT TO BE OUR GREATEST SONG EVER. BUT AXL REALLY DUG IT AS THE LYRICS WERE ABOUT HIS THEN GIRL, ERIN EVERLY, AND WITH IZZY'S ADDED CHORDS... WELL, I GUESS THE RESULT SPEAKS FOR ITSELF. THE WEIRDEST THING IS HEARING MUZAK VERSIONS OF 'SWEET CHILD O' MINE' IN ELEVATORS AND SHOPPING MALLS. I'VE EVEN HEARD AN ARRANGEMENT OF IT FOR THE HARP. RECENTLY I WAS IN A HOTEL AND THE LOUNGE PIANIST WAS PLAYING IT. I GET A MIXTURE OF EMOTIONS WHEN THAT HAPPENS...

Billboard

NATIONAL NEWSWEEKLY OF MUSIC AND HOME ENTERTAINMENT

1 APPETITE FOR DESTRUCTION
Guns N' Roses

2 HYSTERIA
Def Leppard

3 ROLL WITH IT
Steve Winwood

4 TRACY CHAPMAN
Tracy Chapman

5 DIRTY DANCING
Soundtrack

6 OU812
Van Halen

7 FAITH
Geourge Michael

8 HE'S THE D.J., I'M THE RAPPER
D.J. Jazzy Jeff

9 POISON
Say Ahhh..!

10 MORE DIRT

THAT YEAR AXL LOST HIS VOICE FOR A COUPLA DATES AND THE CROWDS GOT REAL ANTSY.

AUGUST 20TH 1988. WE APPEARED AT THE MONSTERS OF ROCK FESTIVAL AT CASTLE DONINGTON IN THE UK. THE CROWD, SAID TO BE UP TO 120,000 PEOPLE, SURGED SEVERAL TIMES DURING OUR SET AND TWO FANS, LANDON SIGGERS AND ALAN DICK, GOT CRUSHED TO DEATH THAT AFTERNOON. WE WERE REALLY BUMMED...

?

THE LIFESTYLE CONTINUED APACE... THE MONEY POURED IN. THE MOUTHS SORTA STAYED SHUT...

I WAS DATING A PORNO CHICK AND ALSO SEEING THIS SWEET LITTLE JAILBAIT JUNKIE GIRL... WE WERE ALL WORRIED ABOUT AIDS... IT WAS LIKE, IF DRINKING DON'T GET ME, AIDS WILL. I EVEN DISCOVERED I HAD BEEN WITH ONE PORNO STARLET WHO HAD APPEARED WITH SEX STAR SUPREMO JOHN HOLMES. I HAVE THIS UNDERLYING FEAR OF MY LACK OF CONTROL...

JACK DANIEL'S THREE-STAR WHISKEY

Rolling Stone

GUNS N' ROSES

HARD-ROCK HEROES

G N'R LIES, OUR SECOND ALBUM, WAS RELEASED IN NOVEMBER AND FEATURED SOME OF THE ACOUSTIC NUMBERS WE HAD LAID DOWN AT THE BEGINNING OF THE YEAR AS WELL AS SOME LIVE?! @ LIKE A SUICIDE TRACKS. IT PROMPTLY ZOOMED TO NUMBER TWO IN THE BILLBOARD CHART... COULD WE DO NO WRONG?

SO, WE ARE NUMBER ONE... THE EL SUPREMOS... I THINK THE ONLY REASON IT COULD HAVE POSSIBLY GONE TO NUMBER ONE IS WE'RE FILLING SOME SORT OF VOID. I KNOW DAMN WELL THAT THE REASON APPETITE IS GOING WHERE IT'S GOING IS BECAUSE WE HIT A CERTAIN FUCKIN' PARTICULAR PLACE AND TIME AND THE SPARKS JUST FLEW... THAT'S REALLY THE ONLY THING I CAN ATTRIBUTE IT TO...

IT'S NOT BECAUSE THE SONGS ARE ALL HUGE HITS. THAT'S THE LAST THING THEY ARE... THEY'RE JUST A BUNCH OF DIRTY ROCK 'N' ROLL SONGS. SO I FIGURE, WE'RE JUST LIKE THE RESIDENT DOWN AND DIRTY ROCK BAND IN TOWN AT THE MOMENT. EVERYBODY WANTS TO HAVE THAT RECORD BECAUSE IT'S NOT REALLY THAT SAFE... AND IT LOOKS COOL NEXT TO THE GEORGE MICHAEL RECORDS IN THEIR COLLECTION. HA HA!

I MEAN, IT'S REALLY NICE TO BE ABLE TO AFFORD AN APARTMENT, AND KNOW WHAT MY FINANCIAL SITUATION IS AND ALL THE REST OF IT. BUT I DON'T NEED ANY OF THAT TO HELP ME WRITE SONGS, AND THAT'S ALL THAT REALLY COUNTS FOR ME.

AFTER FIFTY-SEVEN WEEKS AND APPETITE REACHING NUMBER ONE... WE HAD TWO RECORDS NOW IN THE TOP FIVE... BUT MORE NEGATIVE PUBLICITY RESULTED FROM SOME OF THE LYRICS ON ONE SONG CALLED 'ONE IN A MILLION'.

THE MOST I DO IS, LIKE, ON THE WAY TO THE TROUBADOUR IN 'BOYSTOWN', ON SANTA MONICA BOULEVARD, I'LL YELL OUT THE CAR WINDOW, "WHY DON'T YOU GUYS LIKE PUSSY?" 'CAUSE I'M CONFUSED. I DON'T UNDERSTAND IT. ANTI-HOMOSEXUAL? I'M NOT AGAINST THEM DOING WHAT THEY WANT TO DO AS LONG AS IT'S NOT HURTING ANYBODY ELSE AND THEY'RE NOT FORCING IT UPON ME. I DON'T NEED THEM IN MY FACE OR, PARDON THE PUN, UP MY ASS ABOUT IT...

WHEN I USE THE WORD IMMIGRANTS, I'M TALKING ABOUT GOING TO A 7-ELEVEN OR VILLAGE PANTRY-- A LOT OF PEOPLE FROM COUNTRIES LIKE IRAN, PAKISTAN, CHINA, JAPAN ET CETERA, GET JOBS THERE -- AND THEY TREAT YOU AS IF YOU DON'T BELONG HERE! I'VE BEEN CHASED OUT OF A STORE WITH SLASH BY A SIX-FOOT-TALL IRANIAN WITH A BUTCHER'S KNIFE BECAUSE HE DIDN'T LIKE THE WAY WE WERE DRESSED! ANYWAY, THAT'S WHY I WROTE ABOUT IMMIGRANTS.

MNE

WE KICK-STARTED 1989 AT THE SHRINE AUDITORIUM LA FOR THE AMERICAN MUSIC AWARDS WITH DON HENLEY ON THE DRUM KIT. WE WON THE BEST POP SINGLE WITH 'SWEET CHILD O' MINE'. WE DID A SONG THAT WE REALLY DUG CALLED 'PATIENCE'... AND WE VIDEOED THAT SONG AT THE RECORD PLANT AND THE AMBASSADOR IN TOWN THAT FEBRUARY.

I BEEN WALKIN' THE STREETS AT NIGHT...

YAMAH

THE RUMOUR MILL CONTINUED TO SWIRL AROUND THE BAND. WE WERE CAUGHT IN A MEDIA MAELSTROM THAT WAS HARD TO FATHOM...

WITH THE MONEY CAME THE LAWSUITS, AND ACRIMONY BEGAN TO CREEP INTO THE PICTURE.

I WON'T ALLOW MYSELF TO HAVE A FUCKIN' HABIT... I'LL HAVE DONE BLOW FOR THREE DAYS AND MY MIND WILL GO, "FUCK, NO". I'LL HAVE THE PHYSICAL FEELING OF KNOWING MY BODY NEEDS IT, AND I'LL JUST REFUSE TO DO COKE THAT DAY... BECAUSE IF I WAS GOING TO DO IT, I KNOW I WON'T BE ABLE TO HIT MY GOALS WITH WHAT I WANT TO DO WITH THIS BAND.

THE SAME THING WITH HEROIN. I DID IT FOR THREE WEEKS STRAIGHT AND HAD ONE OF THE GREATEST TIMES IN MY LIFE, BECAUSE I WAS WITH A GIRL I WANTED TO BE WITH IN THIS BEAUTIFUL APARTMENT, AND WE JUST SAT THERE LISTENING TO LED ZEPPELIN, DOING DRUGS AND FUCKING. I STOPPED ON, LIKE, SATURDAY, BECAUSE I HAD SERIOUS BUSINESS TO ATTEND TO ON MONDAY. I FELT LIKE SHIT, SWEATED, SHOOK, BUT ON MONDAY I WAS ABLE TO FUNCTION. I CAN'T HIDE IN DRUGS...

I HAD TO SUE THE GUYS IN COURT TO RECOVER MY EXPENSES. IT'S THE AGE-OLD TALE OF WHAT HAPPENS TO YOU WHEN YOU MAKE IT. WITH THE EXCEPTION OF DUFF THEY WERE ALL LIVING IN MY APARTMENT ON CLARKE STREET IN WEST HOLLYWOOD THROUGH THOSE LEAN YEARS. BUT, Y'KNOW, I'M NOT ALLOWED TO TALK ABOUT IT, I SIGNED A GAGGING ORDER. I'M STILL FRIENDS WITH MOST OF THE BAND...

VICKY HAMILTON WAS A WOMAN WHO BASICALLY HAD A MONOPOLY ON BOOKING BANDS AT THE ROXY AND THE WHISKY, AND WE NEEDED THOSE GIGS. WE ALSO NEEDED A PLACE TO LIVE. SHE SAID SHE'D GET US THE $25,000 WE DESPERATELY NEEDED FOR THE PROPER EQUIPMENT TO START GETTING CLOSE TO THE SOUND WE WANTED...

SHE NEVER CAME THROUGH WITH THE MONEY. SO, WITH AN IMPORTANT GIG COMING UP, WE GOT GEFFEN TO GO FOR A $35,000 MEMO DEAL, WHICH MEANS THAT WE DIDN'T HAVE TO SIGN WITH THEM BUT WE HAD TO PAY THE MONEY BACK.

NOW VICKY'S CLAIMING SHE MANAGED US. SHE CLAIMS SHE INVESTED $100,000 AND SHOULD BE PARTY TO ANY OF THE MONEY WE MAKE. A YEAR LATER SHE SUED US FOR ONE MILLION DOLLARS. WE DIDN'T WANT TO GO TO COURT, PAY LAWYERS' FEES, COURT EXPENSES AND SHIT. POOR VICKY MIGHT LOOK GREAT IN FRONT OF A JUDGE, AND GUNS N' ROSES LOOK LIKE SLIME, SO THEY SHOULD LOSE. WE SETTLED OUT OF COURT FOR $30,000, OF WHICH GEFFEN PAID HALF.

THAT SEPTEMBER DUFF, SLASH AND STEVEN GO TO CHICAGO FOR THREE MONTHS. THEY START TO WORK ON THE NEXT RECORDING BUT NOTHING GETS DONE... BECAUSE AXL AND IZZY DIDN'T SHOW UP IN CHICAGO.

AXL CONTINUED TO EXPLAIN HIS CURRENT STANCE. I DON'T WANT TO SEE DRUGS TEAR UP THIS BAND. I'M AGAINST IT WHEN IT GOES TOO FAR. RIGHT NOW, FOR ME, A LINE OF COKE IS TOO FAR... A LINE OF COKE PUTS MY VOICE OUT OF COMMISSION FOR A WEEK.

WE APPEARED AGAIN AT THE START OF 1990 AT THE AMERICAN MUSIC AWARDS. SLASH MADE A FEW VERBAL FOUR LETTER INROADS DURING HIS ACCEPTANCE SPEECH THAT MADE THE PROCEEDS SIZZLE IN A MORE ROCK 'N' ROLL VEIN...

WE GO IN AND WE JAM AND STUFF AND WE LISTEN TO RAP RECORDS... WE GO THROUGH OUR OWN PERSONAL PROBLEMS AND STUFF... I WANNA THANK ***BLEEP*** TOM ZUTAUT FOR GETTING US THERE...

THE LIFESTYLE CONTINUED APACE. THE MONEY POURED IN. THE MOUTHS STAYED SHUT... SORTA.

...RUMOURS...
...INNUENDO...
...PARANOIA...
...DISTRUST...
...ADDICTIONS...

THAT JULY WE HAD TO FIRE STEVIE. HE JUST COULDN'T CUT IT IN HIS DRUG-ADDLED STATE AND WE FELT BAD. HE HAD DONE HIS LAST SHOW THAT APRIL... HE WAS HOLDING US BACK AND WE HAD TO LET HIM GO.

ON THE WAY TO THE INEVITABLE PARTING OF THE WAYS, STEVEN OD'D WHEN WE WERE FILMING AT *THE FOREST LAWN CEMETERY* FOR POSSIBLE INCLUSION IN THE FILM *THE DEAD POOL.* WE ALL SHOWED UP FOR WHAT WAS SET TO BE SOME GREAT EXPOSURE.

I AM COMING BACK... I AM COMING TO... WHERE WERE WE? I REMEMBER THAT GIRL AND I KINDA REMEMBER THAT HIT...

A PARTING OF THE WAYS IS A SERIES OF EVENTS... A CATALOGUE OF BETRAYALS... A REVERSAL INTO A FOGGY CUL-DE-SAC WITH NO WAY OUT...

MAN, MR BROWNSTONE IS A JEALOUS LOVER AND HE'S DRIVING EVERYONE AND EVERYTHING AWAY FROM ME. MAN, I AM SO STRUNG OUT... BUT, YOU KNOW... THE CALL CAME... I GOT THE CALL...

MAN, THAT WAS CLOSE, STEVE.

OPINIONS VARIED BUT MANAGER ALAN NIVEN WAS FORTHRIGHT: "AS FAR AS I'M CONCERNED, THE BULLSHIT THAT HE WAS FIRED FOR HIS ADDICTION IS JUST THAT -- BULLSHIT. IT WAS A PERFORMANCE MATTER... AND THERE WERE OTHER ISSUES BETWEEN STEVEN AND AXL THAT CERTAINLY DIDN'T HELP AND MAY HAVE BEEN SUFFICIENT IN AND OF THEMSELVES TO SEE HIM GO. I WILL SAY THAT THE BAND NEVER QUITE FELT THE SAME AFTER STEVEN WAS GONE. HE MAY NOT BE THE BEST DRUMMER IN THE WORLD, BUT HE HAD A GREAT EXUBERANCE TO HIS PLAYING WHEN HE WAS 'ON'."

IT WAS CLOSE BUT NO CIGAR FOR STEVEN... HE WAS GIVEN THE BOOT ON JULY 11TH 1990... HE WAS NO LONGER IN *GUNS N' ROSES.* STEVEN HAD ALSO GONE AHEAD AND SIGNED SOME PAPERS IN HIS OUT-OF-IT STATE...

WE WENT AND GOT MATT SORUM IN FROM THE CULT TO PLAY DRUMS. HE PLAYED AND HE HIT FUCKING HARD, WITH A GREAT BASS DRUM KICK TOO. AND HE DIDN'T DO SMACK... HE WAS IN!

AXL GOT MARRIED TO ERIN EVERLY IN LAS VEGAS. THE MARRIAGE LASTED JUST NINE MONTHS... GIVE OR TAKE... EVERYTHING WAS SPEEDING UP AND GETTING HAZY...

CLAIMS WERE MADE THAT DURING AXL'S FREQUENT, UNPREDICTABLE RAGES HE BRANDISHED GUNS, SMASHED ERIN'S BELONGINGS AND YANKED TELEPHONES OUT OF THE WALL.

THERE'S SO MUCH ANGER IN HIM... MAYBE I WAS AN EASY PERSON TO TAKE IT OUT ON... WHAT WAS IT THE LAST TIME? SOMETHING ABOUT MY CLEANING HIS CD COLLECTION? I DIDN'T THINK I COULD SURVIVE MENTALLY ANY LONGER... I WAS DYING INSIDE. AT THE DOOR I TURNED AROUND AND SAID, "I WANT YOU TO LOOK AT ME, BECAUSE YOU'RE NEVER GOING TO SEE ME AGAIN." AND HE NEVER HAS...

FROM AN ASSHOLE!!!
Think of me when you wipe yo' ass...
I am being faithful...
you knew what you got involved
in from the beginning—
Ya didn't need to play it so tough—
I should have known better—
I never realized how much you cared
and wanted me... sometimes I'm an
unsensitive bastard...
To Erin — Sorry yo' birthday sucked,
love, Axl

IN SEPTEMBER WE STARTED RECORDING A NEW ALBUM... EVENTUALLY WE GOT THIRTY-SIX TRACKS IN THE CAN.

WE HAD SOME DIFFICULTY ACHIEVING THE FINAL SOUND OF THE ALBUM, ESPECIALLY DURING THE MIXING STAGES. WE MIXED TWENTY-ONE TRACKS WITH ENGINEER AND PRODUCER BOB CLEARMOUNTAIN, BUT IT DIDN'T SOUND RIGHT SO WE SCRAPPED THE MIXES AND STARTED FROM SCRATCH WITH ENGINEER BILL PRICE OF SEX PISTOLS INFAMY.

Four years later, however, Erin Everly, now 28, is indeed hoping to see Axl Rose, at least one more time— in court. In March she filed a suit in Los Angeles claiming that he had subjected her to physical and emotional abuse. At one point, she alleges, he removed all the doors inside her apartment so that he could monitor her movements. "I was afraid when he came in, when he left, when he wasn't there," she says...

ERROR SM

A GREAT DEAL OF THE MATERIAL FOR THE ALBUM WAS WRITTEN ON ACOUSTIC GUITARS IN A COUPLE OF HOT NIGHTS AT THE WALNUT HOUSE. THIS WAS AFTER SEVERAL MONTHS OF NON-PRODUCTIVITY...

WE APPEARED ON THE OUTSIDE, LOOKING IN THROUGH THE MEDIA WHIRLWIND, TO BE COPING... TO BE A COMPLETE UNIT... BUT THE SAND CASTLE WAS BEGINNING TO FALL INTO THE SEA. ONE PUBLIC FRACAS AFTER ANOTHER ENSUED... *DUFF* GOT INTO A FIGHT AT A GIG AFTER BREAKING UP WITH HIS RECENT WIFE *MANDY BRIXX*... *IZZY* GOT HIS DAY IN COURT ON AN AEROPLANE PUBLIC DISTURBANCE CHARGE, AFTER HE HAD DISRUPTED THE FLIGHT BY PISSING IN THE GALLEY WAY...

THE LIFESTYLE SUFFOCATED US... WAS THIS THE BEGINNING OF THE *END? OUR END?*

IT AIN'T MY IDEA TO TRAVEL IN SEPARATE TOUR BUSES, BUT I CAN'T AFFORD TO PARTY OUT LIKE THE OTHER GUYS. IT'S NOT LIKE WE HAVE OUTGROWN EACH OTHER - WE USED TO LIVE TOGETHER - BUT WE'VE OUTGROWN BEING CROWDED IN TOGETHER...

RUMBO STUDIOS, CANOGA PARK. IT WAS RECORDING TIME FOR REAL. RUMBO WAS A STUDIO THAT PRODUCER MIKE CLINK CHOSE FOR ITS PHYSICAL DISTANCE FROM THE HOLLYWOOD SCENE. CLINK FELT THAT RECORDING THE NOTORIOUSLY RAMBUNCTIOUS AND DESTRUCTIVE GUNS N' ROSES OUT THERE MEANT IT WAS LESS LIKELY THEY'D WANDER OFF AND GET INTO TROUBLE.

WE WERE BECOMING SEPARATED FROM EACH OTHER... WE WERE COLLIDING BUT NOT REALLY CONNECTING...

WE HAD OVER THIRTY SONGS... WAY TOO MANY FOR A SINGLE ALBUM. THE ALBUM WAS TO BE CALLED *USE YOUR ILLUSION*... FROM A PAINTING THAT AXL SAW IN A GALLERY BY A GUY CALLED *MARK KOSTABI.*

ONE SONG HEADING FOR THE ALBUM, 'RIGHT NEXT DOOR TO HELL', WAS ABOUT ANOTHER FRACAS THAT AXL HAD GOTTEN INVOLVED WITH. HE'D BROKEN A WINE BOTTLE OVER HIS NEIGHBOUR'S HEAD... AND THAT ENDED UP IN ANOTHER ARREST DOWN AT WEST HOLLYWOOD POLICE STATION. YET ANOTHER PUBLIC DISTURBANCE...

THE YEAR DISSOLVED INTO ANOTHER AND IN JANUARY 1991, WHILE RECORDING THE ALBUM, WE FOUND TIME TO GO OUT TO ROCK IN RIO AT THE MARACANA STADIUM IN BRAZIL. WE DIDN'T DO ANY INTERVIEWS... WE STAYED ON THE COPACABANA BEACH AT THE PALACE HOTEL. WHEN WE ARRIVED AND GOT OFF THE PLANE IT FELT LIKE WE WERE THE FUCKING BEATLES... WE PLAYED ON TIME AND GOT OUT AND RETURNED HOME.

THIS ALBUM IS GONNA BE DIFFERENT. WHETHER IT'S ACCEPTED OR NOT... I COULDN'T GIVE A SHIT.

MATT SORUM FITTED RIGHT IN. IN FRONT OF 140,000 PEOPLE IN RIO... HE EVEN CAME OUT AND DID A DRUM SOLO.

WE ENDED UP PLAYING TO 260,000 PEOPLE OVER TWO NIGHTS. AXL KEPT THE CROWDS WAITING FOR TWO HOURS AND A NEAR RIOT ENSUED. IN CORCOVADO THE STATUE OF THE REDEEMER LOOKED ON IMPASSIVELY OVER US ALL...

KEEPING AWAY FROM STRIFE IS AN HONOUR FOR A MAN... BUT ANY FOOL WILL QUARREL... PROVERBS 20:3

THAT MAY, ALAN NIVEN, OUR EXTANT MANAGER, GOT FIRED AND DOUG GOLDSTEIN CAME ABOARD IN HIS PLACE. IT WAS SAID THAT AXL FORCED HIM OUT AND WOULD NOT RELEASE THE IMPENDING ALBUM UNTIL HE WAS GONE...

AS SOMEONE IN THE BUSINESS SAID... IF AXL SAYS, "JUMP", GOLDSTEIN SAYS, "FINE"...

NIVEN'S OBSERVATIONS WERE THAT THE PRIMARY FACTORS THAT DESTROYED BANDS WERE WOMEN AND ARGUING OVER DIFFERENTIAL SPLITS OF INCOME, ESPECIALLY MECHANICAL ROYALTIES. HENCE, HE WOULD RECOMMEND EQUAL SHARING OF ROYALTIES, ALTHOUGH NOT WOMEN!

THE FRACTURE BETWEEN AXL AND STEVEN ADLER, FOR EXAMPLE, WAS EXACERBATED BY THESE TWO FACTORS: MONEY AND A WOMAN.

ALL THE PREP WORK FOR ILLUSION AND ITS TOUR, ALL THE RENEGOTIATIONS, EVERYTHING HAD BEEN DONE. SO I WAS THEN DISPENSABLE... SIMPLE, REALLY. I EFFECTIVELY SOLD MY RIGHTS TO ALL PIPELINE AND FUTURE EARNINGS FOR A FRACTION OF THEIR WORTH BACK IN 1991... SUCH WAS MY EMOTIONAL CONDITION AT THE TIME THAT ALL I DESIRED WAS TO BE RID OF ALL FUTURE DEALINGS WITH AXL AND GOLDSTEIN. I WAS IN THE MEADOWLANDS, IN NEW JERSEY, IN 1991... I GOT A PHONE CALL IN THE PRODUCTION OFFICE. IT WAS AXL. HE VERY QUIETLY SAID, "I CAN'T WORK WITH YOU ANYMORE." I SAID, "SORRY TO HEAR THAT. I'LL BE BACK IN LOS ANGELES IN TWO DAYS, LET'S GO OUT AND HAVE DINNER TOGETHER AND TALK ABOUT IT." THAT WAS THE LAST TIME I EVER SPOKE TO HIM. TO THIS DAY, WE'VE NEVER SPOKEN A WORD TO EACH OTHER.

I WAS EMOTIONALLY GROUND DOWN AND FEELING LOW AT THAT POINT. MY ATTITUDE WAS JUST GIVE ME THE CHEQUE SO I DON'T HAVE TO DEAL WITH ANY OF YOU AGAIN. IT SOUNDS LIKE A LOT, BUT $3.5 MILLION WAS MUCH LESS THAN I WAS ALREADY DUE IN SALES OF RECORDS... WAY LESS. AND BY THE TIME YOU GET THROUGH WITH THE IRS AND WITH MY SILENT PARTNERS, IT WAS NOT A LOT OF MONEY... THOUGH I NEVER GOT INTO IT FOR THE MONEY.

SLASH MADE TIME TO PLAY ON MICHAEL JACKSON'S DANGEROUS RECORD, BOTH ON 'BLACK AND WHITE' AND THE SONG 'GIVE IN TO ME'.

I WAS AROUND HIM AND, ALTHOUGH WE WERE THE BIGGEST ROCK STADIUM BAND, HIS STARDOM WAS ON ANOTHER LEVEL. HE WAS WAY OUT THERE... WAY BEYOND WHAT WE WERE DOING OR EXPERIENCING...

DON'T MATTER IF YOU'RE BLACK OR WHITE...

WE HAD THIRTY-SIX SONGS RECORDED AND G N' R STARTED TO THINK ABOUT THE ALBUM TITLE. G N' R SUCKS AND BUY PRODUCT WERE TWO POTENTIAL TITLES, BUT FINALLY THEY DECIDED TO CALL THE ALBUM USE YOUR ILLUSION.

ANOTHER THING TO CONSIDER WAS HOW TO FORMAT THIS... THE 36 SONGS WOULDN'T FIT ON ONE COMPACT DISC. G N' R WANTED TO RELEASE A BOX WITH FOUR CDS BUT GEFFEN SAID NO, IT WOULD BE TOO EXPENSIVE FOR THE FANS. AFTER A LOT OF ARGUING, THEY FINALLY AGREED TO RELEASE TWO CDS ON THE SAME DAY, PLUS ANOTHER CD LATER.

WE FINALLY GOT THE MOTHERFUCKER DONE...

WE GIGGED AND GIGGED AND GIGGED... THE LABEL, THE MANAGEMENT AND THE PROMOTERS WERE WORKING OUR ASSES OFF WHEN YOU'RE HOT, EVERYONE WANTS THAT DOLLAR... THE PRESSURE WAS BUILDING AND BUILDING...

HERE ARE SOME MORE SNAPSHOTS FROM THAT FUCKING CRAZY TOUR. JULY 2ND 1991, WE PLAYED THE RIVERPORT PERFORMANCE ARTS CENTRE, ST LOUIS, MO. AND AXL SPOTTED SOMEONE IN THE CROWD TAKING PICTURES.

AXL AND HIS "LATE" THING STARTED HAPPENING AROUND THEN.

AT A SHOW IN UNIONDALE, NEW YORK ON JUNE 17TH 1991, AXL APOLOGISED TO THE ASSEMBLED THRONG FOR BEING LATE.

YEAH, I KNOW IT SUCKS. IF YOU GOT ANY REAL COMPLAINTS, YOU COULD DO ME A FAVOUR THOUGH... YOU COULD WRITE A LITTLE LETTER ON HOW MUCH THAT SUCKED AND SEND IT TO GEFFEN RECORDS. TELL THOSE PEOPLE TO GET THE FUCK OUT OF MY ASS...

SECURITY DIDN'T RESPOND TO MY REQUEST TO REMOVE THE PERSON. WELL, THANKS TO THE LAME ASS SECURITY, I'M GOING HOME.

THE NEW RECORD WILL BE DELAYED AGAIN. GEFFEN RECORDS DECIDED THEY WANTED TO CHANGE THE CONTRACT AND I'M DECIDING FUCK YOU... AND SINCE I DON'T HAVE TIME TO DO BOTH, GO BACK THERE AND ARGUE AND BITCH WITH THEM OR BE ON TOUR AND HAVE A GOOD TIME AND FUCK THEM. IT'S A SHAME, BUT... SO WE'LL PLAY A LOT OF THE NEW SHIT TONIGHT AND IT REALLY DOESN'T MATTER, DOES IT?

HEY!! BEAT THE LIVING FUCK OUT OF ANYBODY WHO THROWS SOMETHING AT THE STAGE. I WON'T BE THROWING ANYTHING BACK INTO THE CROWD, I'LL JUST LEAVE...

ON THE 13TH AUGUST 1991 THE GET IN THE RING MOTHERFUCKER TOUR CAME TO EUROPE. WE ARRIVED IN SWEDEN AND AXL WAS GETTING MORE AND MORE WEIRDED OUT. AT THE FIRST OF TWO SHOWS HELD AT THE JÄÄHALLI IN HELSINKI WITH SKID ROW OPENING FOR US...

...ABOUT AN HOUR INTO THE SHOW, AS THE BAND LAUNCH INTO 'WELCOME TO THE JUNGLE', AXL UPS AND LEAVES THE STAGE.

WE FOLLOWED AXL OFF STAGE AND A FUCKING RIOT BROKE OUT. WE WANTED TO GO BACK ON, BUT WE WERE ADVISED NOT TO. OUR EQUIPMENT GOT CONFISCATED AND AXL WAS CHARGED WITH INCITING A FULL-ON RIOT.

A FREAKIN' CODE 100 WAS PUT OUT FOR A FULL-SCALE RIOT... 500 FULLY GEARED UP POLICE OFFICERS ARRIVED THERE. THEY WERE FIRING ON THE UNRULY MOB WITH FIRE HOSES AND CAPSTUN, WHICH IS KINDA LIKE MACE. IT CAME TO A COOL $200,000 WORTH OF DAMAGES.

WE CARRIED ON PLAYING AN INSTRUMENTAL VERSION OF THE SONG AND CONTINUED THE SET WITH '14 YEARS', A DRUM SOLO AND THEN A GUITAR SOLO... AFTER 25 MINUTES, AXL RETURNED TO THE STAGE. THE ATMOSPHERE WAS TENSE ALL THE TIME WITH AXL AND HIS PHALANX OF BODYGUARDS.

SECURITY, I'M GOING HOME...

THINGS ESCALATED AND GOT WORSE. WE WERE PHOTOGRAPHED BY THE SWEDISH PAPER EXPRESSEN AND THAT DIDN'T GO DOWN WELL. THE BODYGUARDS TRIED TO STOP IT BUT FAILED. AT LEAST THE PAPER GAVE THE SHOWS FIVE OUT OF FIVE. WE HAD ALREADY SOLD OUT THE GLOBEN IN STOCKHOLM... IT TOOK JUST FOUR HOURS TO SELL 13,000 TICKETS FOR THE SHOW.

WE ARE SOOOOO HOT MAN... THIS TOUR IS GONNA KILL THIS BAND OR ONE OF US IS GONNA DIE REAL SOON...

OUR GIG ON 17TH AUGUST STARTED REAL LATE AGAIN BECAUSE OF AXL'S HUBRIS... ON THE WAY TO THE GIG, HE STOPPED AND PLAYED ROULETTE FOR ONE AND A HALF HOURS. LATER ON THE BUS HAD TO STOP TO LET HIM WATCH THE FUCKING STOCKHOLM FIREWORKS. WE EVENTUALLY HIT THE STAGE AT ELEVEN O' CLOCK.

THIS IS CALLED 'KNOCKIN' ON HEAVEN'S DOOR'... NOW ON THIS ONE, MAYBE YOU PEOPLE THAT HAVE BEEN FALLING ASLEEP THE WHOLE FUCKIN' SHOW COULD SING ALONG TOO. IF YOU'RE BORED, YOU SHOULD'VE SAVED YOUR MONEY AND GONE AND SEEN THE FIREWORKS TONIGHT.

A COUPLE OF DAYS LATER, THE SHOW WAS HELD UP BECAUSE AXL COULDN'T HANDLE THE FACT THAT SOMEONE HAD THROWN A FIRECRACKER ON THE STAGE. AFTER FIFTEEN MINUTES THE SHOW RESUMED... MORE HUBRIS.

20TH AUGUST. WE ARRIVED IN OSLO, BUT WHERE WAS AXL? HE JUST DISAPPEARED... NOBODY KNEW WHERE HE WAS AT ALL. THE BAND WENT AHEAD AND CHECKED IN AT THE GRAND HOTEL.

21ST AUGUST. WE GET THE CALL THAT AXL IS IN PARIS... LATER, AT FIVE OR SIX IN THE DAMN MORNING, WE HEARD THAT HE AIN'T GONNA MAKE THE SHOW LATER TONIGHT. THE SHOW AT SPEKTRUM IN OSLO IS CANCELLED...

THAT AUGUST WE PLAYED FINLAND, SWEDEN, DENMARK AND GERMANY AND ENDED UP AT WEMBLEY STADIUM, LONDON. WE SOLD OVER 38,000 TICKETS IN TWO DAYS. WE WERE SELLING TICKETS QUICKER THAN THE STONES AND MADONNA.

GUNS N' F***ING ROSES

WEMBLEY F***ING STADIUM

SOLD F***ING OUT

IN SEPTEMBER THE USE YOUR ILLUSION ALBUMS WERE RELEASED... AND BY 5TH OCTOBER 1991, USE YOUR ILLUSION II WAS AT NUMBER ONE WITH A BULLET ON THE BILLBOARD TOP 200 ALBUMS CHART. THE ALBUM SPENT THE NEXT TWO WEEKS AT THE TOP OF THE CHART.

DRUMMERS CAN GO ALL NIGHT

THE CRAZINESS KEPT GETTING RAMPED UP IN SO MANY WAYS AND STEVE ADLER FILED A LAWSUIT AGAINST THE BAND FOR BOTH DEFAMATION OF CHARACTER AND DEFRAUDING HIM. HE CLAIMED THE BAND WERE RESPONSIBLE FOR HIS ADDICTIONS... HE WAS SUING TO THE AMOUNT OF TWO MILLION DOLLARS.

I WAS THEIR SCAPEGOAT... THEY WERE DOING DRUGS AND SO WAS I, AND I DIDN'T THINK I WAS DOING ANYTHING WRONG. I BELIEVE IN MY FIVE YEARS WITH THEM I WAS ENCOURAGED TO TAKE HEROIN... DOUG GOLDSTEIN CALLED ME INTO THE OFFICE ABOUT TWO WEEKS LATER... HE WANTED ME TO SIGN SOME CONTRACTS.

I WAS TOLD THAT EVERY TIME I DID HEROIN, THE BAND WOULD FINE ME $2,000... THERE WAS A WHOLE STACK OF PAPERS, WITH COLOURED PAPER CLIPS EVERYWHERE FOR MY SIGNATURES. WHAT THESE CONTRACTS ACTUALLY SAID WAS THAT THE BAND WERE PAYING ME $2,000 TO LEAVE... THEY WERE TAKING MY ROYALTIES, ALL MY WRITING CREDITS. THAT'S WHY I FILED THE LAWSUIT -- TO GET ALL THOSE THINGS BACK...

IN THE COMBAT ZONE ANOTHER MEMBER BOWED OUT. MANY FELT IZZY STRADLIN WAS THE TRUE HEART AND SOUL OF GUNS N' ROSES. AXL, FOR HIS PART, THOUGHT IZZY WAS COASTING AND HE AND SLASH WERE PUTTING IN ALL THE EFFORT ONSTAGE. THE GIG ON AUGUST 31ST 1991 AT WEMBLEY WAS TO BE IZZY'S LAST SHOW AS A FULL MEMBER OF G N' R.

I JUST DON'T WANT TO DO IT ANYMORE... THE MONEY, SEX, THE STADIUMS, THE AUDIENCES, THE ACCLAIM NOT-WITHSTANDING.

WE SOON LOST ANOTHER INTEGRAL AND IRREPLACEABLE PART OF GUNS N' ROSES. ON NOVEMBER 7TH 1991, IZZY STRADLIN LEFT GUNS N' ROSES. HIS SOON-COME REPLACEMENT WAS GILBY CLARKE, WHO HAD BEEN PLAYING THE SAME CLUBS AS G N' R.

I WAS LIKE, IS THIS ALL THERE IS? I WAS JUST TIRED OF IT... I NEEDED TO GET OUT. I DIDN'T LIKE THE COMPLICATIONS THAT BECAME SUCH A PART OF DAILY LIFE IN GUNS N' ROSES. FOR EXAMPLE, THE RIVERPORT RIOT AND AXL ROSE'S CHRONIC LATENESS ON THE USE YOUR ILLUSION TOUR. I STARTED GETTING SOBER AND WHEN YOU'RE FUCKED UP YOU'RE MORE LIKELY TO PUT UP WITH THINGS YOU WOULDN'T NORMALLY PUT UP WITH...

AXL WANTED TO ADD A KEYBOARDIST CALLED DIZZY REED...
MAYBE TO HELP WITH VOCAL TUNING AND PITCHING.

APRIL 6TH 1992. THE MYRIAD ARENA IN OKLAHOMA CITY.
WE ARRIVED BACK AFTER GIGGING IN MEXICO.

DO YOU BELIEVE ALL THE SHIT YOU READ? DO YOU EVER WONDER WHY YOU'RE GIVEN SO MUCH SHIT TO READ? YOU'RE GIVEN A LOT OF SHIT TO READ, BECAUSE THERE'S A LOT OF FUCKING PEOPLE OUT THERE WHO I DON'T THINK I SHOULD EVEN GIVE THEM THE CREDIT TO SAY THAT THEY'RE VERY CONSCIOUS OF WHAT THEY'RE DOING. BUT IT'S MAINLY BECAUSE THEY DON'T WANT THINGS LIKE THIS CONCERT HERE IN OKLAHOMA TO FUCKING HAPPEN. YEAH, THERE'S A LOT OF PEOPLE WHO DON'T KNOW WHY THEY DO THINGS, BUT SOME OF THE REASONS BEHIND THAT... THEY DON'T WANT PEOPLE LIKE YOU, THAT ARE HERE TONIGHT, TO SEE SOME LITTLE LOUD MOUTHY FUCKER LIKE ME. THERE'S SOMETHING OUT THERE THAT DOESN'T WANT PEOPLE LIKE YOU TO REALISE THAT YOU CAN DO WHATEVER THE FUCK YOU WANT WITH YOUR GODDAM LIFE...

THEY CAN SUCK MY DICK...

I BELIEVE THAT DEEP INSIDE EVERYBODY, THERE'S SOMETHING THAT KNOWS WHAT THE FUCK YOU'RE SUPPOSED TO TO WITH YOUR LIFE... AND NO MATTER WHAT ANYBODY TELLS YOU, IF YOU KEEP LOOKING AND YOU KEEP DIGGING YOU'RE GONNA FIND IT... AND I KNOW IT'S NOT LIKE THE MOST HUMANE THING, BUT YOU CAN, WHEN IT GETS REAL ROUGH, THINK OF A THEME SONG THAT SOME-BODY ELSE WROTE. NAMELY MR PAUL MCCARTNEY... AND WHEN THEY'RE TRYING TO KEEP YOU DOWN, JUST HOLD ON AND KNOW SOMEDAY YOU'LL BUST OUT, YOU'LL GET ONTO YOUR OWN SHIT AND THEY WON'T BE ABLE TO FUCKING KEEP UP WITH YOUR ASS...

AND YOU CAN BE THINKING JUST LIVE AND LET DIE MOTHERFUCKER...

WE KEPT DRAWING THE BIGGEST CROWDS. AT THE CANNSTATTER WASEN IN STUTTGART, GERMANY ON MAY 27TH 1992, 75,000 PEOPLE SHOWED UP. WE WARMED THEM UP BY ANNOUNCING, "OK YOU BEER SWILLING, MERC DRIVING MUGS..."

I'M TRYING TO GET OFFA THE SAUCE... I'M FEELING ANTSY BUT I'M GOING TO KEEP TRYING...

JUNE 20TH 1992, WURZBURG, GERMANY. ONE OF THE WORST STORMS IN RECENT YEARS HITS THE SITE. 45,000 FANS WITNESS AN ASTONISHING SHOW DURING WHICH THE LIGHTNING CANNOT BE DISTINGUISHED FROM THE ONSTAGE PYROTECHNICS. BOTH THE CROWD AND THE BAND ARE TOTALLY SOAKED TO THE SKIN... THE STEAM RISING FROM THOSE PACKED AT THE FRONT PREVENTS THOSE FURTHER BACK FROM EVEN SEEING THE STAGE...

WE WERE SETTING UP DATES WITH METALLICA FOR A TOUR THAT WAS TO START THAT COMING JULY, BUT BEFORE THAT AXL WAS ARRESTED...

NEW GUY GILBY CLARKE WAS FITTING IN AND THE BAND APPEARED TO BE GELLING AGAIN. HE HAD A GOOD INTENSIVE GUITAR EDUCATION WITH THE BANDS KILL FOR THRILLS, BLACKOUTS AND CANDY.

ACCORDING TO SLASH, I WAS THE ONLY GUY THEY AUDITIONED. DAVE NAVARRO OF THE CHILI PEPPERS WAS IN THE FRAME FOR A HOT MINUTE AND HE WAS TALKING TO AXL, BUT HE LIKED HIS DRUGS AND THAT WAS THE LAST THING THEY NEEDED. I HAD THE LOOK, THE VIBE AND THE SKILLS NEEDED...

OUR NEXT ALBUM WAS GETTING READY FOR RELEASE... OUR FIFTH. IT WAS JOKILY NAMED THE SPAGHETTI INCIDENT... AFTER A FOOD FIGHT THAT AXL AND STEVE ADLER HAD WITH EACH OTHER. MUCH WAS MADE OF THIS FOOD FIGHT DURING ADLER'S LAWSUIT AGAINST THE BAND LATER IN 1993, IN WHICH ADLER'S ATTORNEY REFERRED TO IT AS "THE SPAGHETTI INCIDENT".

AXL WAS BECOMING MORE AND MORE ISOLATED AND WITHDRAWN. SLASH AND AXL WERE POLARISING AND GROWING VERY DISTANT. NEW MANAGER DOUG GOLDSTEIN SEEMED TO BE A YES MAN... EXCLUSIVE TO AXL AND NOT REPRESENTING THE BAND AS A WHOLE ENTITY...

IT WAS AROUND THEN THAT WE ALL BEGAN TO SPLIT WITH AXL... HE WAS TOTALLY ON ANOTHER PAGE. THERE WAS A BIG, BIG GAP... WE WEREN'T A BAND ANYMORE, JUST A BUNCH OF GUYS WHO MET UP ONSTAGE. I THINK EVERYONE THOUGHT THEY SHOULD HAVE LEFT ALONG WITH IZZY.

PARANOIA LEVELS GREW TO AN ALL TIME HIGH (OR LOW). AXL GOT HIMSELF SOMEONE DESCRIBED AS A 'PSYCHIC' AND SHE ADDED TO THE BURGEONING ENTOURAGE SURROUNDING THE BAND. HER NAME WAS SHARON MAYNARD AND SHE BECAME A FIXTURE ON THE TOURS AND IN THE GUNS N' ROSES CAMP SHE WAS QUICKLY NICKNAMED YODA AFTER THE STAR WARS CHARACTER...

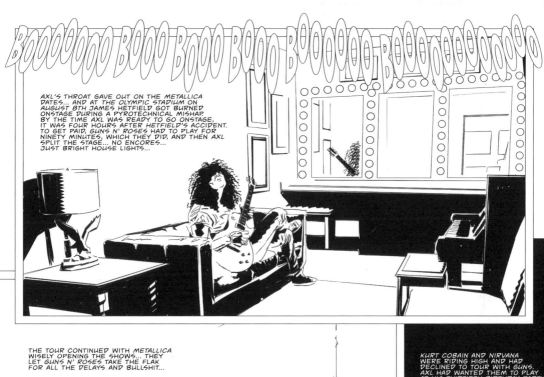

BOOOOOOO BOOO BOOO BOOO BOOOOOO BOOOOOOOOO

AXL'S THROAT GAVE OUT ON THE METALLICA DATES... AND AT THE OLYMPIC STADIUM ON AUGUST 8TH JAMES HETFIELD GOT BURNED ONSTAGE DURING A PYROTECHNICAL MISHAP. BY THE TIME AXL WAS READY TO GO ONSTAGE, IT WAS FOUR HOURS AFTER HETFIELD'S ACCIDENT. TO GET PAID, GUNS N' ROSES HAD TO PLAY FOR NINETY MINUTES, WHICH THEY DID, AND THEN AXL SPLIT THE STAGE... NO ENCORES... JUST BRIGHT HOUSE LIGHTS...

THE TOUR CONTINUED WITH METALLICA WISELY OPENING THE SHOWS... THEY LET GUNS N' ROSES TAKE THE FLAK FOR ALL THE DELAYS AND BULLSHIT...

THE BAND LOST NEARLY 80% OF THE TOUR REVENUES DUE TO UNION OVERTIME FEES AND CURFEW FINES.

WE'RE ALWAYS FUCKING HAMMERED BEFORE WE GET ONSTAGE. ALL THE WAITING... YOU HAVE A DRINK TO CALM DOWN... THEN ANOTHER... THEN ANOTHER... DUFF WAS IN TERRIBLE SHAPE. HE COULD BARELY MOVE SOMETIMES...

KURT COBAIN AND NIRVANA WERE RIDING HIGH AND HAD DECLINED TO TOUR WITH GUNS. AXL HAD WANTED THEM TO PLAY AT HIS THIRTIETH BIRTHDAY PARTY, BUT KURT COBAIN HAD REFUSED OUTRIGHT. HE HAD "PISSED" THEM, TOO, IN THE PRESS ACCORDING TO AXL. AXL HAD HIS OWN RETORTS. ONE SUCH DELIVERED FROM THE STAGE APPEARED IN VANITY FAIR, IN WHICH AXL WAS REPORTED TO HAVE SAID, "KURT COBAIN IS A FUCKING JUNKIE WITH A JUNKIE WIFE. AND IF THE BABY'S BORN DEFORMED, I THINK THEY BOTH OUGHT TO GO TO PRISON."

THEY ARE PEOPLE WITH NO TALENT. THEY WRITE THESE CRAP SONGS AND THEY'RE THE MOST POPULAR BAND ON THE PLANET RIGHT NOW. I CAN'T BELIEVE IT...

BOURBON COUNTY

AT THE 1992 MTV VIDEO MUSIC AWARDS, AXL AND COURTNEY LOVE AND KURT COBAIN ALMOST GOT INTO IT..

IT SEEMS ALL THESE GUYS HAD IN COMMON WAS A SMALL TOWN MISFIT UPBRINGING...

HEY, AXL! WILL YOU BE THE GODFATHER OF OUR CHILD?

VMA

AXL INSISTED ON TELLING KURT WHAT HE NEEDED TO DO.

YOU SHUT YOUR BITCH UP OR I'M TAKING YOU DOWN TO THE PAVEMENT.

OKAY BITCH... SHUT UP!

HAAAA HA HA AHA AHA!

THAT SORTA BACKFIRED ON AXL... MADE HIM LOOK RUNTISH AND OUT OF TOUCH WITH THE NEW GUARD REPRESENTED BY NIRVANA. AXL, WITH STEPHANIE SEYMOUR IN TOW, LEFT THE THRONG WITH LAUGHTER RINGING IN THEIR EARS.

KURT LATER REMARKED, "WE THOUGHT HE WAS JUST A STUPID JOKE!"

THE METALLICA CO-TOUR MOVED ON... FAITH NO MORE GOT DUMPED OFFA THE TOUR AND FOR THE LAST FIVE SHOWS MOTORHEAD AND LA RAP GROUP BODY COUNT TOOK UP THE SLACK.

MY VOCAL CHORDS ARE TAKING A HAMMERING RIGHT NOW... I'M WONDERING WHETHER I'M GOING TO LAST THIS TOUR OUT! I ALREADY HAD TO THROW THREE SHOWS IN JULY EARLIER THIS YEAR WHEN MY VOCE WENT.

THIS LINEUP PLAYED IN SAN FRANCISCO THAT SEPTEMBER AND IT WAS THERE THAT SLASH DIED! SLASH HAD INVITED SOME JUNKIE FRIENDS TO THE AFTER-SHOW PARTY AT THE HOTEL. THEY HAD JUNK AND THEY HAD COCAINE, TOO... AND SLASH WAS HEADING TO MATT SORUM'S HOTEL ROOM...

THIS WAS AROUND 6AM IN THE MORNING AND SLASH COLLAPSED IN THE CORRIDOR.

HE JUST TURNED BLUE AND DIED... OUT FOR NEARLY EIGHT MINUTES... THE ADRENALINE SHOTS JOLTED HIM BACK TO LIFE.

I HAD NO REMORSE AT THE OD... BUT I WAS PISSED AT MYSELF FOR HAVING DIED.

WE KEPT THE TOUR GOING ALL THROUGH THAT YEAR... TAKING IN FURTHER SOUTH AMERICAN DATES IN VENEZUELA, COLUMBIA, CHILE AND ARGENTINA.

ALL THE CANCELLATIONS... NO-SHOWS AND LATE GIG ONSTAGE ARRIVALS WERE STARTING TO EAT INTO THE TOUR'S OVERALL MORALE. METALLICA AND JAMES HETFIELD WERE GETTING ENTIRELY SICK OF G N' R, PARTICULARLY AXL AND HIS DEMANDS...

AXL POSE, WHAT AN ASSHOLE, JUST COMPLETE CHICKENSHIT... THE PIDDLING NEEDS AND WANTS OF CERTAIN PEOPLE ON THE ROAD... READING THIS FUCKER'S BACK-STAGE RIDER DEMANDS MAKES ME WANT TO HURL...

AXL HAD ONE DIRECT WAY OF DEALING WITH THE PAPARAZZI'S CONSTANT DEMANDS... SOME IN YOUR FACE AVERSION THERAPY...

ASSHOLES... HERE... TAKE THESE AFTER THEY FUCKING HIT YOUR HEAD... YOU CAN SIT ON 'EM.

TO CELEBRATE THE CONSTANT FIGHTING AND UPROAR IN THEIR RELATIONSHIP STEPHANIE SEYMOUR AND AXL GOT ENGAGED IN EARLY 1993. HOWEVER, AXL, SUSPECTING SOME INFIDELITY, FORCED STEPHANIE TO LEAVE THEIR HOUSE THAT MARCH...

THINGS GOT SERIOUS AND THE ENGAGEMENT WAS DISSOLVED. AXL WAS CITING HE WANTED THE RETURN OF $100,000 WORTH OF JEWELLERY, PLUS SHE HAD ASSAULTED HIM BY ATTACKING HIS GENITALIA THAT PRECEDING CHRISTMAS.

SHE'S ALSO BRINGING IN ERIN EVERLY TO TESTIFY ON HER BEHALF... I'M HERE ALL ALONE IN MALIBU.

AS THE TOURING BLED INTO A NEW YEAR... GILBY BROKE HIS WRIST IN A MOTORCYCLE ACCIDENT AND COULD NOT DO ANY OF THE IMPENDING DATES. BOTH SLASH AND AXL AGREED TO GET IZZY BACK IN. IZZY CAME BACK REJUVENATED AND FRESH FROM HIS JU JU HOUNDS PROJECT. IT'S SAID THAT IZZY GOT A MILLION FOR THE NEXT FIVE SHOWS... NICE WORK IF YOU CAN GET IT...

INTO 1993 AND THE TOURING CONTINUES UNABATED... GET IT WHILE IT'S HOT. JANUARY THROUGH TO JULY... ONE OF THE LONGEST TOURS IN ROCK HISTORY. TWENTY-SEVEN COUNTRIES AND 192 DATES IN ALL... PLAYING TO OVER SEVEN MILLION PEOPLE AND GROSSING A REPORTED SIXTY MILLION DOLLARS.

JANUARY
FEBRUARY
MARCH
APRIL
MAY
JUNE
JULY

AUGUST 23RD 1993, LOS ANGELES SUPERIOR COURT. AXL IS HERE TO TESTIFY AGAINST STEVEN ADLER. THE OCTOBER 1991 LAWSUIT HAD FINALLY COME TO COURT.

STEVEN COULDN'T PLAY DUE TO HIS DRUG ABUSE. FOR EXAMPLE, HIS DRUM TRACK FOR THE SONG 'CIVIL WAR' HAD TO BE EDITED TOGETHER FROM OVER 60 TAKES.

AROUND THEN AXL ALSO HAD A BEEF WITH STEVEN ADLER DUE TO A SEEMING DRUG SITUATION INVOLVING HIS EX-WIFE-TO-BE ERIN.

THERE WAS MORE BACK STORY TO THIS... BACK THEN WHEN I GOT KICKED OUT OF G N' R... ERIN EVERLY HAD COME BY OUR PLACE, SHE WAS IN TOW WITH AN ACT I WAS HANGING WITH, A CAT CALLED ANDY MCCOY, GUITARIST FROM HANOI ROCKS. SHE WAS HIGH, OR AT LEAST SEEMED IT... ERIN SAID SHE AND AXL HAD ANOTHER FIGHT. PEOPLE WHO WERE THERE WERE TELLING ME TO GIVE HER SOMETHING. I DIDN'T AND WE CALLED THE MEDICS... SHE GOT PUMPED AND IT SEEMS THERE WAS SMACK IN HER SYSTEM.

AXL BLAMED ME AND WANTED TO KILL ME.

SEPTEMBER 24TH 1993. GUNS N' ROSES MADE A 2.5 MILLION DOLLAR OUT-OF-COURT SETTLEMENT PAYMENT TO STEVEN ADLER IN RESPECT OF HIS OCTOBER 1991 LAWSUIT... PLUS HE GOT 15% OF ROYALTIES DATED PRIOR TO HIS DEPARTURE. THAT WAS THE UPSIDE. THE DOWNSIDE? STEVEN WENT ON A DRUG BINGE THAT RESULTED IN A STROKE LEAVING HIM PERMANENTLY SPEECH-IMPAIRED.

NOVEMBER 23RD 1993. THE COVER ALBUM, "THE SPAGHETTI INCIDENT?", IS RELEASED IN THE US. ONE OF THE SONGS IS 'LOOK AT YOUR GAME GIRL', WRITTEN BY ONE CHARLES MANSON. IT IS CONSIDERED IN REMARKABLY BAD TASTE AND CAUSES SOME CONTROVERSY...

APPARENTLY AXL AND THE GUYS DID NOT KNOW THIS WAS A MANSON TUNE, BUT IT WAS THE REJECTION OF THIS SONG BY THE RECORD LABELS BACK IN 1969 WHICH HAD SPARKED OFF HIS MURDEROUS SPREE IN THOSE INFAMOUS LA KILLINGS.

THINK YOU'RE LOVIN' BABY... AND ALL YA DO IS CRYIN'...

THE REST OF SPAGHETTI INCIDENT FEATURED GREAT RAW PUNK COVERS THAT THE BAND DUG... MATERIAL LIKE 'NEW ROSE' BY THE DAMNED, 'RAW POWER' BY IGGY AND THE STOOGES, 'YOU CAN'T PUT YOUR ARMS AROUND A MEMORY' BY JOHNNY THUNDERS AND OTHER SPECIALLY PICKED TRACKS...

JANUARY 20TH 1994. AXL APPEARS AND INTRODUCES THE INDUCTION OF HIS MUSICAL INSPIRATION ELTON JOHN INTO THE ROCK AND ROLL HALL OF FAME. LATER THAT NIGHT, AXL PERFORMS 'COME TOGETHER' WITH BRUCE SPRINGSTEEN.

MUSIC HELPS US GET THROUGH EACH DAY OF OUR LIVES. TO ME, NO ONE HAS BEEN THERE FOR ME LIKE ELTON JOHN... WHEN WE THINK OF GREAT DUOS I THINK OF ELTON JOHN AND BERNIE TAUPIN.

MAY 1994 AND DUFF IS CLOSE TO DEATH WHEN HIS PANCREAS EXPLODES. THE HEALTH CRISIS IS TRIGGERED BY HIS INTENSE AND PROLONGED ABUSE OF DRUGS AND ALCOHOL. ALCOHOL CAN BE CONSIDERED A LESSER EVIL THAN POWDERS, BUT IT CAN BRING RUIN JUST AS BAD... MAYBE MORE SLOWLY IS ALL.

I LOOK LIKE A BLOATED ELVIS. I WAS IN HOSPITAL FOR TEN DAYS. THE END OF MY DRINKING CAREER CAME WHEN MY PANCREAS BURST, WHICH WAS NOT FUN... IT LETS OUT THE BILE, WHICH GIVES YOUR STOMACH AND INTESTINE THIRD DEGREE BURNS. USUALLY THEY SLIT YOU OPEN TO LET SOME OF THE STEAM OUT, WHICH RELIEVES THE PAIN BEFORE YOU DIE. MY PANCREAS WAS APPARENTLY SWOLLEN TO THE SIZE OF A FOOTBALL FROM ALL THE BOOZE. I HAD THIRD-DEGREE BURNS ALL OVER THE INSIDE OF MY BODY FROM THE DIGESTIVE ENZYMES RELEASED BY THE DAMAGED PANCREAS... IT WAS TIME FOR A TOTAL CHANGE.

DUFF HIGHTAILED IT BACK TO SEATTLE FOR SOME RECOVERY TIME. HIS COMPANION BACK HOME WAS KURT COBAIN, A FATED INDIVIDUAL RETURNING AFTER CHECKING OUT OF THE LATEST REHAB PROGRAMME. SHORTLY AFTER THIS KURT PLACED A SHOTGUN IN HIS MOUTH. DID HE END HIS OWN MISERY IN A FINAL ACT OF SELF-INFLICTED MERCY?

I WAS ON MORPHINE FOR MY PANCREAS AND TAKING OTHER STUFF TO CONTROL THE ALCOHOLIC DELIRIUM TREMENS. GUESS KURT HAD GONE MUCH FURTHER DOWN HIS APPOINTED LINE TO HIS APPOINTED TIME.

I WAS IN MY HELL, HE WAS IN HIS, AND WE BOTH SEEMED TO UNDERSTAND. WHEN WE ARRIVED IN SEATTLE AND WENT TOWARD THE BAGGAGE CLAIM, THE THOUGHT CROSSED MY MIND TO INVITE HIM OVER TO MY PLACE. I HAD A SENSE HE WAS LONELY AND ALONE THAT NIGHT. SO WAS I, BUT THERE WAS A MAD RUSH OF PEOPLE IN THE TERMINAL... I WAS IN A BIG ROCK BAND; HE WAS IN A BIG ROCK BAND... WE COWERED NEXT TO EACH OTHER AS PEOPLE GAWKED. I LOST MY TRAIN OF THOUGHT FOR A MINUTE, AND KURT SLIPPED OUT TO A WAITING LIMO. KURT RODE THE SMACK TRAIN ALL THE WAY INTO THE TWILIGHT BONEYARD...

THAT JUNE, GILBY CLARKE IS GIVEN NOTICE AND SUMMARILY FIRED.

THAT KIND OF STUFF, THE RUMOURS... YOU CAN NEVER STOP IT. I'VE HEARD SO MANY REPORTS THAT I GOT FIRED AND, YOU KNOW, I'VE BEEN IN THE BAND FOR TWO-AND-A-HALF YEARS, AND I'VE BEEN FIRED A FEW TIMES. ALL KINDS OF PEOPLE HAVE BEEN FIRED!

FOR REAL, I'VE SEEN MORE THAN JUST ME BEING FIRED. I'VE SEEN OTHER PEOPLE QUIT, I'VE SEEN OTHER PEOPLE FIRED, YOU KNOW, WHATEVER... IT'S NOT THAT BIG A DEAL REALLY IN THE WHOLE G N' R WORLD. YOU DON'T KNOW WHAT'S GOING TO HAPPEN... FROM THE DAY I GOT THE JOB, I DIDN'T KNOW IF I'D BE THERE FOR A WEEK, A YEAR, WHATEVER...

BUT THE ROYALTIES STOPPED SO I RELUCTANTLY SUED. IF YOU JIVE YOU SUFFER THE CONSEQUENCES. WE SETTLED OUTTA COURT...

AXL WENT AWOL...
OR AT LEAST TO
THE PUBLIC HE
DISAPPEARED
FOR ALMOST
FOUR YEARS.

THERE WERE RECORDINGS
DONE AT THE COMPLEX, BUT
AXL WOULD ONLY SHOW AT
TWO IN THE MORNING. HE
WAS WATCHFUL AND
DISENGAGED... THE BAND
WOULD GET BORED AND
LEAVE HIM TO RECORD
ALONE.

AXL BECAME PUBLIC NEWS AGAIN ON FEBRUARY 11TH 1998. HE IS ALLEGED TO HAVE ASSAULTED A SECURITY WORKER AT PHOENIX SKY HARBOR AIRPORT.

AXL ROSE WAS ON HIS WAY THROUGH THE SOUTHWEST AIRLINES BAGGAGE CHECK WHEN HE ALLEGEDLY OBJECTED TO HAVING HIS LUGGAGE SEARCHED BY AIRPORT SECURITY PERSONNEL. "HE BEGAN TO YELL THREATS AND OBSCENITIES AT THE GUARD," SAID SGT KENT DEBNAM OF THE PHOENIX POLICE DEPARTMENT, READING FROM A REPORT OF THE INCIDENT IN WHICH ROSE ALLEGEDLY SHOUTED, "I'LL PUNCH YOUR LIGHTS OUT RIGHT HERE AND RIGHT NOW," WHILE ALLEGEDLY SHAKING HIS FISTS AT THE SECURITY WORKER.

AXL COPPED TO A MISDEMEANOUR CHARGE, PLEADING GUILTY FOR DISTURBING THE PEACE. HE HAD BEEN TRANSPORTED TO THE MARICOPA COUNTY JAIL BEFORE HIS BAIL WAS POSTED.

THE EMPIRE THAT WAS STARTED IN 1985 WAS CRUMBLING... SIGNS OF THE FALL WERE EVERYWHERE.

I GOT MY BAND SLASH'S SNAKEPIT TOGETHER IN THE INTERIM AND WE PLAYED HARD. I ALSO APPEARED ONSTAGE WITH MICHAEL JACKSON.

AND CONFUSION CAME TO REIGN IN THE EMPIRE...

RIGHT NOW, AXL AND I ARE DELIBERATING OVER THE FUTURE OF OUR RELATIONSHIP AND THE WHOLE GUNS N' ROSES THING.

THE NEWLY CROWNED KING OF THIS EMPIRE, AXL SAID THAT SLASH WAS NOT A PART OF THE GUNS N' ROSES BAND.

AXL SENT A FAX TO MTV THAT SAID SLASH HADN'T BEEN A PART OF G N' R SINCE 1995 AND, DESPITE THIS STARTLING FACT, THAT THERE WILL BE A NEW G N' R RECORD.

AXL ROSE BUYS THE RIGHTS TO THE NAME GUNS N' ROSES. NO CONFUSION AS TO WHO IS THE BOSS NOW.

YEAH -- ABOUT BUYING THE NAME AND RIGHTS... THAT'S SOMETHING THAT HAPPENED. I WAS BLINDSIDED BY IT, MORE OR LESS A LEGAL FAUX PAS. I DON'T KNOW WHAT HE'S GONNA DO, AS FAR AS THAT GOES, BUT I'D BE LYING TO SAY I WASN'T A LITTLE BIT PEEVED AT THAT. IT'D BE ONE THING IF I QUIT ALTOGETHER, BUT I HAVEN'T. IT'S THE FACT THAT HE CAN ACTUALLY GO AND DO THAT WITHOUT THE CONSENT OF THE OTHER MEMBERS OF THE BAND...

AXL ROSE BUYS THE GUNS N' ROSES NAME

AXL AND I HAVE JUST NOT BEEN ABLE TO HAVE A MEETING OF THE MINDS SO THAT WE CAN ACTUALLY WORK TOGETHER... WE'VE BEEN THROUGH THIS A DOZEN TIMES. IT SEEMS LIKE A BIG DEAL NOW, BUT TO ME IT'S MORE OF THE SAME. I HAVEN'T REALLY GONE ANYWHERE... I HAVEN'T OFFICIALLY QUIT THE BAND. IT'S JUST THAT WE'RE NOT SEEING EYE-TO-EYE ON WHERE GUNS SHOULD BE GOING. IT'S JUST SUCH A PAIN IN THE ASS...

BY AUGUST 1997 DUFF HAD HAD ENOUGH...

I WENT OUT FOR DINNER WITH AXL AND TOLD HIM, "ENOUGH IS ENOUGH". THIS BAND IS A DICTATORSHIP AND I DON'T SEE MYSELF PLAYING UNDER THOSE CONDITIONS... GO FIND SOMEONE ELSE.

DUFF FOUND HIMSELF GETTING TOGETHER WITH THE SEX PISTOLS' STEVE JONES, DURAN DURAN'S JOHN TAYLOR AND EX-GUNS N' ROSES DRUMMER MATT SORUM TO FORM HEAVY METAL SUPER-GROUP THE NEUROTIC OUTSIDERS.

WE HUNG OUT AT THE VIPER ROOMS AND DECIDED TO FORM A KINDA SUPER-GROUP.

THE NEUROTIC OUTSIDERS PLAYED THE CLUB SCENE BEFORE RELEASING A SELF-TITLED ALBUM ON MAVERICK RECORDS AND GOING ON TOUR THROUGH EUROPE AND SOUTH AMERICA.

WE DISBANDED IN 1997 BUT I ALSO GOT ANOTHER GROUP THING TOGETHER CALLED LOADED, WHICH STILL PERFORMS TO THIS DAY...

AXL WAS TO UNVEIL NEW SONGS... AND A NEW AXL INTERVIEW WAS PUBLISHED IN *ROLLING STONE*. AXL MENTIONED SOME NEW SONG TITLES IN THE MAKING... 'CATCHER IN THE RYE', 'THE BLUE'S', 'I.R.S' AND 'TWAT'.

SLASH TO ME HAD LOST HIS 'DIVE IN AND FIND THE MONKEY' TYPE OF ATTITUDE. IT WAS TIME FOR FRESH INPUT...

JOHN FREESE CAME INTO THE BAND ON DRUMS. HE CO-WROTE A SONG CALLED 'CHINESE DEMOCRACY'... THAT NAME, OR THAT TITLE, WOULD RING LOUD IN GEFFEN RECORDS' EARS FOR SOME TIME TO COME...

I'M HERE, BUT FOR HOW LONG?

DURING THIS TIME, GEFFEN RECORDS PAID ROSE A MILLION DOLLARS TO TRY TO FINISH THE ALBUM... WITH A FURTHER ONE MILLION DOLLARS IF HE HANDED IT IN TO THEM BY MARCH 1ST 1999. IT WAS TWICE NO DICE.

IN REGARD TO SO-CALLED PERFECTIONISM, I FEEL THAT HAS A LOT TO DO WITH YOUR GOALS OR REQUIREMENTS, WITH WHATEVER ONE'S DOING OR CREATING... DIFFERENT LEVELS MAY BE REQUIRED FOR DIFFERENT OBJECTIVES. IF YOU'RE MAKING BRAKES FOR A VEHICLE, WHAT'S REQUIRED? IT'S ALL RELATIVE, RIGHT? YOU TRY TO MAKE THE BEST CALLS YOU CAN AT ANY GIVEN MOMENT AND GO FROM THERE. GENERALLY WHEN THIS TERM IS USED BY OTHERS IN REGARD TO ME OR HOW I WORK, IT'S SAID IN A NEGATIVE WAY OR AS AN EXCUSE FOR THEIR SHORTCOMINGS... AND AGAIN BY MY DETRACTORS...

SLASH FOUND HIS HOME STUDIO THE SNAKEPIT TO BE A PLACE OF CALM AND SANCTUARY AFTER THE GUNS MADNESS AND RELENTLESS TOURING. HE HAD PRESENTED SOME TUNES TO AXL, BUT THEY WERE REJECTED AT FIRST... AND THEN LATER REQUESTED.

Y'KNOW, IT IS ALWAYS FIVE O'CLOCK SOMEWHERE... I WANTED TO REMAIN INCOGNITO AS I PUT OUT MY OWN RECORD, BUT THE LABEL NEEDED MY NAME ON THERE TO SELL IT...

LOWER THAN THE BOTTOM... SWALLOWED BY THE RIDE...

I DID REHAB AND I KICKED SMACK AGAIN... IT WAS GETTING HARDER AND THE WITHDRAWALS WERE DIFFICULT, MAN. I COULD NOT EAT, WATCH TV OR NOTHING. REHAB WAS GOOD AND AFTER A WEEK OR SO THE SWEATS AND ANXIETY STARTED TO WANE. I DIDN'T MAKE IT THAT TIME. I HAD TO PICK UP AND TRY THE OLD GAME AGAIN... IT TOOK A FEW GOES BEFORE I GOT IT...

TOUGH WINDS BLEW THROUGH THE MUSIC BUSINESS... GEFFEN GOT FOLDED INTO INTERSCOPE, THINGS GOT BIG AND CORPORATE... EVEN MORE SO THAN BEFORE. LOTS OF LABEL EXECS HAD LOST THEIR JOBS ON BLACK FRIDAY... YOU COULD SEE THOSE GUYS WALKING SUNSET WITH THEIR OFFICE BOXES.

I BOUGHT MY RECORD BACK. I DIDN'T TRUST THE GUY AT INTERSCOPE... THE MUSIC INDUSTRY IS A SPRING-LOADED MINEFIELD... YOU BETTER WATCH OUT. BUT I GOT OUT AND GIGGED WITH MY BAND SNAKEPIT...

WILD HOOOORSES, COULDN'T DRAG ME AWAAAAYYY...

THE TURN OF THE CENTURY. THE YEAR 2000 AND AXL UNVEILS A "NEW" GUNS N' ROSES. A CAT CALLED JOSH FREESE HAD BEEN IN ON DRUMS BUT WAS NOW GONE, REPLACED BY A NEW GUY CALLED BRAIN (AKA BRYAN MANTIA). ANOTHER GUY, ROBIN FINCK FROM NINE INCH NAILS, WAS ON GUITAR... HE REPLACED SLASH. PLUS THERE WAS ANOTHER MYSTERIOUS DUDE CALLED BUCKETHEAD... MORE OF HIM IN A MINUTE.

AXL STARTS THE NEW DECADE WITH AN IMPROMPTU GIG AT THE CAT CLUB ON SUNSET STRIP. AXL SINGS WITH THE THURSDAY NIGHT HOUSE BAND THE STARFUCKERS. SLIM JIM PHANTOM WAS IN THE BAND AND SO WAS DEPARTED G N' R GUITARIST GILBY CLARKE. AXL SAT IN, SOCIALISED, THEN SPLIT...

THE NEW RECORDING IS TO BE CALLED CHINESE DEMOCRACY. IT'S KINDA LED ZEPPELIN MEETS TRENT REZNOR STROKE ELECTRONICA MUSIC.

MOBY WAS CALLED ON TO HELP WITH THE EVOLVING ALBUM PROJECT, AS NOTHING HAD BEEN HEARD SINCE THE SPAGHETTI INCIDENT. THEY ALSO GOT ANOTHER UK PRODUCER GUY IN CALLED YOUTH...

I SPENT A COUPLE OF DAYS IN THE STUDIO WITH HIM, AND IT WAS VERY INTERESTIN I'M FLOWN OUT TO LOS ANGEL TO SIT IN THE STUDIO WITH AX I KNOW THIS IS GOING TO SOUND BUT I FOUND HIM TO BE REALLY OF A SENSITIVE, SLIGHTLY TROUL PERSON. I WISH HIM WELL AND I THAT AT SOME POINT THEY FINISH RECORD AND THAT IT'S GREAT. I WO FEEL COMFORTABLE DESCRIBING MUSIC AT ALL. THERE'S GOING TO A TECHNO INFLUENCE, BUT IT W STILL BE RECOGNISABLE AS G N' R... IT'S NOT AXL'S INTENTION TO CUT SOME WHOLLY NEW CLOTH...

HE SEEMED EMOTIONAL RESERVED A A LITTLE B SUSPICIOUS HE SEEMED LITTLE BIT LI A BEATEN DOG.

THE RECORDING WAS GOING TO BE A LONG WAIT FOR THE RECORD COMPANY... A LONG WAIT FOR EVERYONE. BUT THE BAND GOT OUT AND GIGGED.. AND THE SHOWS WERE STILL SELLING OUT. INTERSCOPE WERE SUGGESTING A 2001 RELEASE DATE FOR THE NEW ALBUM.

"HIS WORLD IS VERY INSULAR," SAYS DOUG GOLDSTEIN. "HE DOESN'T LIKE VERY MANY PEOPLE."

AXL HAS OPENED UP IN THE PAST ABOUT HIS EXPERIENCES WITH PAST-LIFE REGRESSION THERAPY. THE SESSIONS BEGIN WITH HYPNOSIS... DURING TRADITIONAL PSYCHOTHERAPY, A PATIENT PLACED IN A TRANCE MAY BE ABLE TO RECALL TRAUMATIC EVENTS THAT HAVE BEEN REPRESSED AND MAY LIE AT THE ROOT OF CURRENT EMOTIONAL PROBLEMS...

A PATIENT MAY BE ABLE TO REMEMBER BACK EVEN FURTHER, TO A LIFE OR LIVES THAT WERE LIVED HUNDREDS IF NOT THOUSANDS OF YEARS AGO. PATIENTS MAY SPEAK IN THE VOICE OR THE LANGUAGE OF SOME LONG-DEAD BEING. AXL, ACCORDING TO A CONFIDENTIAL SOURCE, BELIEVES HE AND STEPHANIE SEYMOUR WERE TOGETHER IN FIFTEEN OR SIXTEEN PAST LIVES...

PEOPLE ARE SAYING IT IS A SOLO RECORD BUT THAT'S NOT WHE I'M GOING HERE. THER RUMOURS ABOUT IT BE A TECHNO RECORD... E IT'S WHAT GUNS N' RO HAVE ALWAYS BEEN. DIVERSIFIED.

THE BAND RETURNED TO RIO DE JANEIRO, BRAZIL, AND THREE HOURS AFTER THE GOO GOO DOLLS FINISHED THEIR SET, AXL WENT ONSTAGE...

GOOD MORNING... I'VE JUST WOKE UP. I HAVE BEEN TAKING A NAP FOR EIGHT YEARS... I KNOW YOU WANT THE OLD BAND. SOME OF THE PEOPLE YOU CAME TO KNOW AND LOVE COULD NOT BE WITH US HERE TODAY. REGARDLESS OF WHAT YOU HAVE HEARD OR WHAT PEOPLE HAVE SAID... PEOPLE WORKED VERY HARD... I MEAN MY FORMER FRIENDS... TO DO EVERYTHING THEY COULD SO THAT I COULD NOT BE HERE TODAY. I SAY, FUCK THAT!

THE SPECTRE OF SLASH'S LINGERING CHARISMA SEEMED TO VEX AXL CONTINUOUSLY. HE COULD NOT LET IT RIDE OR LET IT DROP.

SLASH AND MCKAGAN DID MORE DAMAGE TO ABILITY AS A WRITER... THEM, IT WAS ALL CRAP. EAT ME DOWN SO MUCH E TIME OF THE USE YOUR N TOURS. SLASH AND DUFF "YOU'RE AN IDIOT. YOU'RE OSER." I DIDN'T WRITE FOR YEARS. I FELT I WAS HINDERED FOR A VERY LONG TIME...

WE ENDED IN FRONT OF 100,000 PEOPLE... WE WENT OUT GOOD. BY THE END IT WAS JUST SMOKE AND MIRRORS... WE WERE RUNNING ON EMPTY FUMES, MAN. I WAS GIVEN A CONTRACT TO JOIN HIS NEW BAND. IT TOOK ME ABOUT TWENTY-FOUR HOURS BEFORE I DECIDED. I THINK THIS IS THE END OF THE LINE... I'M DONE.

DECEMBER 31ST 2001. GUNS N' ROSES PLAY THE JOINT IN LAS VEGAS, NEVADA... WITH THE YEAR ENDING ON A SLASH UNFRIENDLY NOTE.

IT WAS SAID THAT SLASH WANTED TO COME IN BACKSTAGE...

WE DIDN'T KNOW WHAT HIS INTENTIONS WERE. IF NOTHING ELSE IT WOULD HAVE BEEN A DISTRACTION. AXL WAS REALLY NERVOUS ABOUT THESE SHOWS. WE DECIDED ON OUR OWN NOT TO TAKE ANY RISK.

BUCKETHEAD (AKA BRIAN CARROLL) CAME IN AND REPLACED ROBIN FINCK, WHO HAD REPLACED SLASH. MR BUCKET WAS A MYSTERIOUS INDIVIDUAL ENCASED IN A KFC CHICKEN BUCKET AND A MASK, HENCE HIS APT MONIKER.

BEAMED IN FOR CHINESE DEMOCRACY... BERMUDA TRIANGLE... ELECTRIC TEARS... FUNNEL WEAVER?

MORE DEBACLES AS THE NEW TOUR GROUND ON... G N' R PLAY THE LEEDS FESTIVAL IN ENGLAND ON AUGUST 23RD 2002. THE SHOW STARTS AT 11:10PM, AN HOUR LATER THAN SCHEDULED BECAUSE OF DELAYS CAUSED BY TECHNICAL PROBLEMS. IT SEEMS THE CITY COUNCIL WANT TO INTERFERE, BUT GUNS N' ROSES WERE ALLOWED TO FINISH THEIR SET.

WELL, IT APPEARS THAT WE'RE GONNA HAVE AN INTERESTING EVENING. YOU SEE, THE CITY COUNCIL AND THE PROMOTERS SAY WE HAVE TO, LIKE, END THE SHOW. AND THEY COULD SAY MAYBE I'M INCITING A RIOT. NOW I'M NOT, 'CAUSE I DON'T WANT ANYONE TO GET ARRESTED OR ANYONE TO GET IN TROUBLE OR ANYTHING LIKE THAT, BUT I THINK WE GOT A GOOD SEVEN OR EIGHT FUCKIN' SONGS LEFT AT LEAST... AND I DIDN'T FUCKIN' COME ALL THE WAY OVER TO FUCKIN' ENGLAND TO BE TOLD TO GO BACK FUCKIN' HOME BY SOME FUCKIN' ASSHOLE! ALL I'VE GOT FOR THE LAST EIGHT YEARS IS SHIT AFTER SHIT AFTER SHIT IN THE FUCKIN' PRESS AND AXL'S THIS, AXL'S THAT. I'M HERE TO PLAY A FUCKIN' SHOW AND WE WANNA PLAY! SO, IF YOU WANNA STAY, I WANNA STAY AND WE'LL SEE WHAT HAPPENS... EVERYBODY... NOBODY TRY TO GET IN TROUBLE OR ANYTHING. TRY TO HAVE A GOOD TIME...

PEOPLE ARE ASKING WHAT'S UP WITH AXL'S VOCALS AT THE MTV MUSIC VIDEO AWARDS SHOW ON AUGUST 29TH 2002.

HE SOUNDED WAY OFF... BREATHLESS AND SOMEWHAT TUNED OUT...

CLASSIC ROCK MAGAZINE CALLED IT "THE GREATEST G N' R TRIBUTE BAND IN THE WORLD".

THE NO-SHOWS CONTINUED... GENERAL MOTORS
PLACE ARENA, VANCOUVER AND THE FIRST TOUR
NIGHT... TEN THOUSAND ANGRY AND RESTLESS
PEOPLE WAITED FOR THE BAND. AXL WASN'T
EVEN IN THE COUNTRY FOR THE GIG...

MANAGEMENT SENT OUT A DISCLAIMER
SAYING THAT THE GIG WAS CANCELLED
WHEN AXL AND THE BAND WERE STILL
IN THE AIR AND FURTHER DELAYED AT
THE AIRPORT, ETCETERA. THE ENSUING
RIOT CAUSED SEVERAL THOUSAND
DOLLARS WORTH OF DAMAGE TO THE
VENUE AND POLICE HAD TO USE
PEPPER SPRAY AND ATTACK DOGS TO
QUELL THE CROWD.

THE VANCOUVER GIG BECAME AN
OFF-LIMITS INTERVIEW TOPIC AND
AXL EVEN WANTED PRE-APPROVED
COPY ON ALL INTERVIEWS. THE
EMPIRE CONSTRICTED AND
TIGHTENED UP ITS ACT.

INTERVIEWERS WERE
ENCOURAGED TO TALK
ABOUT THE FORTH-
COMING CHINESE
DEMOCRACY ALBUM.

STEVE ADLER WAS GAINING GROUND WITH HIS NEW BAND SUKI JONES... WHO EVENTUALLY MORPHED INTO ADLER'S APPETITE. HE FORMED THE BAND IN LA IN 2003 WITH KERI KELLI FROM SNAKEPIT. THEY WERE TO PLAY GREAT VERSIONS OF SONGS FROM THE APPETITE FOR DESTRUCTION ALBUM.

MY SUBSTANCE ABUSE ISSUES HAVE CONTINUED... AT TIMES, I USED UP TO $3000 WORTH OF DRUGS IN ONE NIGHT. I COULDN'T STAND BEING UP WHEN THE SUN CAME UP. I KNEW I HAD NOTHING TO DO... MY PHONE DIDN'T RING FOR YEARS, EXCEPT FOR THE DRUG DEALER CALLIN' ME BACK...

THIS IS ADLER'S APPETITE TOUR. I'M DOING THE SAME THING AXL WAS DOING, EXCEPT IT'S MORE FUN. I'M GIVING FANS ONE ORIGINAL MEMBER AND PLAYING EVERY SONG THE PEOPLE WANT. I ALSO RECENTLY REKINDLED MY FRIENDSHIP WITH SLASH... I'VE BEEN SO HAPPY GETTING MY FRIEND BACK. I MISSED HIM SO MUCH...

SLASH WAS BUSYING HIMSELF TOO... HIS NEW BAND VELVET REVOLVER WAS REVEALED ON JUNE 19TH 2003 AT A LIVE SHOW AT THE EL REY THEATRE IN LOS ANGELES. THE EXCLUSIVE INVITATION-ONLY GIG WAS PRECEDED BY A MEDIA QUESTION-AND-ANSWER SESSION. THE SETLIST INCLUDED 'BODIES' BY THE SEX PISTOLS, 'SET ME FREE', 'SEX TYPE THING' BY THE STONE TEMPLE PILOTS, 'IT'S SO EASY' BY GUNS N' ROSES, 'SLITHER' AND 'NEGATIVE CREEP' BY NIRVANA...

THAT AUGUST VELVET REVOLVER SIGNED WITH RCA RECORDS AND THEIR PRESS BLURB DECLAIMED... WE'RE THRILLED TO PARTNER WITH RCA RECORDS AND ITS LEGENDARY CHIEF, THE ENIGMATIC CLIVE DAVIS... WE BELIEVE THIS MARRIAGE WILL BE A LOYAL, DEDICATED AND FRUITFUL RELATIONSHIP NOT BASED SOLELY ON BUSINESS, BUT INSTEAD ON THE THING THAT ONCE DARED US ALL TO DREAM... MUSIC.

I WAS DEFINITELY IN A RUT EMOTIONALLY AND SPIRITUALLY. I'D FALLEN OFF THE WAGON PRETTY HARD, AND I WAS VERY DEPRESSED... A SUICIDAL DEPRESSION. I WAS SEPARATED FROM MY WIFE, I'D REALLY TOTALLY DISTANCED MYSELF FROM ALL MY FRIENDS AND I WAS COMPLETELY ISOLATED, LIVING IN MY L.A. HOUSE BY MYSELF. THE ONLY PERSON I SAW WAS MY DRUG DEALER... IT WAS INCREDIBLY LONELY, AND I REALLY DIDN'T SEE A WAY OUT OF IT, YOU KNOW? SO, LIKE, WHEN THE VELVET REVOLVER OPPORTUNITY PRESENTED ITSELF, I WAS FORCED TO BE AROUND PEOPLE WHO HAD A POSITIVE OUTLOOK ON THINGS. IT KIND OF GAVE ME A DIFFERENT WAY TO LOOK AT THINGS, ALTHOUGH I WAS STILL IN IT AT THE TIME...

LOOKS LIKE SCOTT WAS ALSO STILL "IN IT". THAT OCTOBER 27TH, WEILAND WAS ARRESTED IN BURBANK ON CHARGES OF DRIVING UNDER THE INFLUENCE OF ALCOHOL AND DRUGS AND ALSO A MISDEMEANOR HIT-AND-RUN FOLLOWING A TRAFFIC COLLISION THAT OCCURRED IN HOLLYWOOD. HE WAS ORDERED TO REPORT TO A LIVE-IN DETOX PROGRAMME, FOLLOWED BY SIX MONTHS IN A RESIDENTIAL DRUG REHAB CENTRE.

THE ARREST MARKED THE FOURTH TIME WEILAND HAD BEEN BUSTED ON DRUG CHARGES. HE'D PREVIOUSLY BEEN COLLARED IN CALIFORNIA IN 1995 AND 1997, AND NEW YORK IN 1998. IN 1999 HE SERVED A STINT IN PRISON WHEN A LOS ANGELES JUDGE RULED THAT THE SINGER HAD VIOLATED THE TERMS OF HIS PROBATION WITH A HEROIN OVERDOSE, AND IN 2001 HE WAS ARRESTED IN LAS VEGAS ON A DOMESTIC VIOLENCE CHARGE, INVOLVING HIS WIFE.

THEY FUCKIN' HAD MY BACK... TOTALLY, SELFLESSLY, THOSE GUYS WERE THERE FOR ME. NONE OF THESE FUCKERS STAB MY BACK. THERE'S NO, LIKE, "YOU MOTHERFUCKER, WHY DO YOU DO THE THINGS YOU DO?" LIKE, I'M SURROUNDED WITH A GROUP OF GUYS THAT ARE ALL FUCKING JUNKIES, YOU KNOW?

THEY'VE DONE EVERYTHING THAT I'VE DONE TO THE HILT, SO THERE'S NO JUDGMENT THERE. MY LAST FIX WAS THE MORNING AFTER I GOT OUT OF JAIL, JUST TO GET MYSELF WELL. I WENT TO THE DOCTOR AND PICKED UP SOME MEDICATION TO KICK WITH, AND DUFF AND DAVE FLEW ME UP TO SEATTLE... WE WENT UP TO THE MOUNTAINS.

WHO HATH WOE? WHO HATH SORROW? WHO HATH CONTENTIONS? WHO HATH BABBLING? WHO HATH WOUNDS WITHOUT CAUSE? WHO HATH REDNESS OF EYES? PROVERBS 23:29

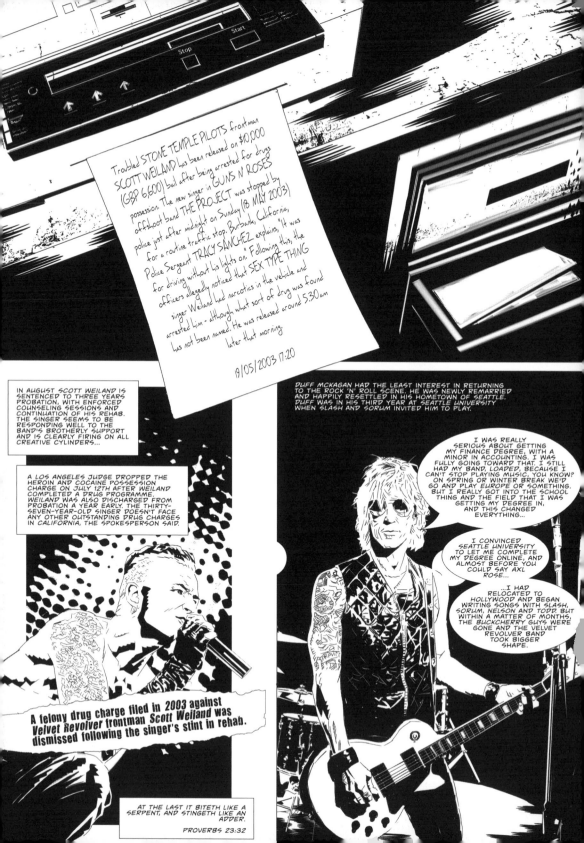

Troubled STONE TEMPLE PILOTS frontman SCOTT WEILAND has been released on $10,000 (GBP 6,600) bail after being arrested for drugs possession. The new singer in GUNS N' ROSES' offshoot band THE PROJECT was stopped by police just after midnight on Sunday (18 MAY 2003) for a routine traffic stop. Burbank, California, Police Sergeant TRACY SANCHEZ explains, "It was for driving without his lights on." Following this, the officers allegedly noticed that SEX TYPE THING singer Weiland had narcotics in the vehicle and arrested him - although what sort of drug was found has not been named. He was released around 5.30 am later that morning.

19/05/2003 17:20

IN AUGUST SCOTT WEILAND IS SENTENCED TO THREE YEARS PROBATION, WITH ENFORCED COUNSELING SESSIONS AND CONTINUATION OF HIS REHAB. THE SINGER SEEMS TO BE RESPONDING WELL TO THE BAND'S BROTHERLY SUPPORT AND IS CLEARLY FIRING ON ALL CREATIVE CYLINDERS...

A LOS ANGELES JUDGE DROPPED THE HEROIN AND COCAINE POSSESSION CHARGE ON JULY 12TH AFTER WEILAND COMPLETED A DRUG PROGRAMME. WEILAND WAS ALSO DISCHARGED FROM PROBATION A YEAR EARLY. THE THIRTY-SEVEN-YEAR-OLD SINGER DOESN'T FACE ANY OTHER OUTSTANDING DRUG CHARGES IN CALIFORNIA, THE SPOKESPERSON SAID.

A felony drug charge filed in 2003 against Velvet Revolver frontman Scott Weiland was dismissed following the singer's stint in rehab.

AT THE LAST IT BITETH LIKE A SERPENT, AND STINGETH LIKE AN ADDER.

PROVERBS 23:32

DUFF MCKAGAN HAD THE LEAST INTEREST IN RETURNING TO THE ROCK 'N' ROLL SCENE. HE WAS NEWLY REMARRIED AND HAPPILY RESETTLED IN HIS HOMETOWN OF SEATTLE. DUFF WAS IN HIS THIRD YEAR AT SEATTLE UNIVERSITY WHEN SLASH AND SORUM INVITED HIM TO PLAY.

I WAS REALLY SERIOUS ABOUT GETTING MY FINANCE DEGREE, WITH A MINOR IN ACCOUNTING. I WAS FULLY GOING TOWARD THAT. I STILL HAD MY BAND, LOADED, BECAUSE I CAN'T STOP PLAYING MUSIC, YOU KNOW? ON SPRING OR WINTER BREAK WE'D GO AND PLAY EUROPE OR SOMETHING. BUT I REALLY GOT INTO THE SCHOOL THING AND THE FIELD THAT I WAS GETTING MY DEGREE IN, AND THIS CHANGED EVERYTHING...

I CONVINCED SEATTLE UNIVERSITY TO LET ME COMPLETE MY DEGREE ONLINE, AND ALMOST BEFORE YOU COULD SAY AXL ROSE...

...I HAD RELOCATED TO HOLLYWOOD AND BEGAN WRITING SONGS WITH SLASH, SORUM, NELSON AND TODD. BUT WITHIN A MATTER OF MONTHS, THE BUCKCHERRY GUYS WERE GONE AND THE VELVET REVOLVER BAND TOOK BIGGER SHAPE.

MARCH 15TH 2004. GREATEST HITS IS RELEASED IN EUROPE. THE ALBUM GOES TO NUMBER ONE IN AT LEAST NINE EUROPEAN COUNTRIES.

MARCH 23RD 2004: US RELEASE OF GREATEST HITS AND THE ALBUM ENTERS THE BILLBOARD CHART AT NUMBER THREE.

GEFFEN RECORDS ALSO LET AXL KNOW THE FOLLOWING... THAT "HAVING EXCEEDED ALL BUDGETED AND APPROVED RECORDING COSTS BY MILLIONS OF DOLLARS" IT WAS NOW "MR ROSE'S OBLIGATION TO FUND AND COMPLETE THE ALBUM, NOT GEFFEN'S".

AS ALWAYS, YOU COULD NOT PLEASE ALL THE PEOPLE ALL OF THE TIME... CERTAINLY NOT THE PEOPLE IN THIS CONVOLUTED EPIC.

AXL ROSE IMMEDIATELY TRIED TO BLOCK THE GREATEST HITS RELEASE BY SUING GEFFEN, SAYING IT WOULD RUIN HIS FOCUS ON CHINESE DEMOCRACY AND RISKED LEAVING THE NEW ALBUM UNNOTICED.

FORMER BAND MATES SLASH AND DUFF MCKAGAN HELPED AXL ROSE FILE THE LAWSUIT AGAINST GEFFEN, ALTHOUGH THEY DID NOT SPEAK TO EACH OTHER IN PERSON. THE SUIT FAILED AND THE ALBUM WAS RELEASED.

FANS ALSO CRITICISED THE TRACK LISTING, CITING THE LACK OF SOME POPULAR SONGS AND TOO MANY COVER VERSIONS.

THE NEXT ROCK IN RIO WAS FAST APPROACHING, BUT ANOTHER IMPORTANT MEMBER BAILED OUT. GUNS N' ROSES WERE SCHEDULED TO HEADLINE A FESTIVAL IN LISBON, PORTUGAL ON MAY 30TH. IT IS UNCLEAR WHETHER THE BAND WILL HAVE A NEW GUITARIST BY THEN...

GUITARIST BUCKETHEAD HAD HAD ENOUGH. HE WAS IN G N' R FOR FOUR YEARS, DURING WHICH TIME THE BAND CANCELLED MORE SHOWS THAN IT PLAYED AND RELEASED NO ORIGINAL MATERIAL.

OCTOBER 12TH 2004. G N' R ISSUED THE FOLLOWING PRESS RELEASE REGARDING RUMOURS THAT THEY HAD RECRUITED A NEW GUITARIST TO REPLACE BUCKETHEAD.

"THERE HAVE BEEN NUMEROUS REPORTS OVER THE LAST FEW WEEKS FROM VARIOUS SOURCES CLAIMING THAT ONE PERSON OR ANOTHER HAS BEEN INVITED TO JOIN GUNS N' ROSES. TO SET THE RECORD STRAIGHT NO ONE – WE REPEAT NO ONE – HAS BEEN INVITED TO JOIN THE BAND. WE WOULD NORMALLY NOT RESPOND TO RUMOURS BUT IT IS WRONG TO ALLOW A FEW SELF-PUBLICISTS THE PLATFORM TO MISLEAD THE MEDIA AND GUNS N' ROSES FANS. WE WILL LET YOU KNOW WHEN THERE IS CREDIBLE NEWS ON THIS SUBJECT."

A PRESS RELEASE WAS PUT OUT. WAS THIS DESCRIBING BUCKETHEAD OR SOMEONE ELSE CLOSER TO HOME?

"DURING HIS TENURE WITH THE BAND, BUCKETHEAD HAS BEEN INCONSISTENT AND ERRATIC IN BOTH HIS BEHAVIOUR AND HIS COMMITMENT... DESPITE BEING UNDER CONTRACT, CREATING UNCERTAINTY AND CONFUSION AND MAKING IT VIRTUALLY IMPOSSIBLE TO MOVE FORWARD WITH RECORDING, REHEARSALS AND LIVE PLANS WITH CONFIDENCE. HIS TRANSIENT LIFESTYLE HAS MADE IT NEAR IMPOSSIBLE FOR EVEN HIS CLOSEST FRIENDS TO HAVE NEARLY ANY FORM OF COMMUNICATIONS WITH HIM WHATSOEVER..."

ON APRIL 29TH 2004 A LAWSUIT IN WHICH DUFF AND SLASH SUED AXL, CLAIMING THEY WERE RIPPED OFF TO THE TUNE OF AT LEAST A MILLION DOLLARS, WAS FILED AT THE LOS ANGELES SUPERIOR COURT.

KFC
FUNERAL

LOS ANGELES COUNTY SUPERIOR COURT

NEW GUITAR FIREPOWER WAS NEEDED TO FILL *BUCKETHEAD'S* SHOES... SO AXL HIRED RON *'BUMBLEFOOT'* THAL.

I STARTED CHATTING WITH THE G N' R FOLKS IN THE SUMMER OF 2004, BUT WE DIDN'T GET ACTIVE UNTIL THEY HAD A TOUR STARTING IN MAY 2006. AXL AND I MET FACE-TO-FACE FOR THE FIRST TIME JAMMING TO THE SONG 'RIAD N' THE BEDOUINS' IN NEW YORK IN APRIL 2006, A FEW DAYS BEFORE THE TOUR BEGAN. I JAMMED SEVEN TIMES WITH THE BAND AND WE HIT THE ROAD... BY THE WAY MY NICKNAME IS BASED ON A BACTERIAL INFECTION... KINDA NEAT, HUH?

NOW G N' R HAD THREE GUITAR SLINGERS... WERE SLASH'S SHOES THAT HARD TO FILL? WITH BUMBLEFOOT, ROBIN FINCK AND RICHARD FORTUS, AXL WAS NOT TAKING ANY CHANCES ON THE LIVE BAND FRONT.

AXL WAS NOW FORTY-FOUR YEARS OLD... CARRYING A HEAVIER FRAME... BUT PEOPLE WERE STILL EMBRACING THE BAND ECSTATICALLY.

HARD TO HOLD A CANDLE IN THE COLD NOVEMBER RAIN...

THE CLASSIC LINE-UP WERE ALL PLOUGHING THEIR VARIOUS FURROWS... IN STEVEN'S CASE HIS FOREHEAD WAS FURROWED... ANXIETY-LINED WITH ALL OF THE ONGOING ADDICTIONS.

I WAS GOING TO GO BACK TO LAS VEGAS AND GET A HOUSE... I WANTED TO BE NEAR MY MOM. I WAS STILL DANCING WITH THE DEVIL... I AVOIDED GOING NEAR HEROIN... BUT CRACK COCAINE WAS A HARSH MISTRESS...

I WAS A WALKING CORPSE, MAN... I WAS DOWN T[O] A HUNDRED AND FIFTE[EN] POUNDS. SLASH AND [MY] BROTHER JAMIE, WHO [HAD] BEEN DOING AA, CAME [OVER] AND DID AN INTERVENT[ION] MAN. I WAS PISSED, B[UT] THEY WERE TRYING [...] TO SAVE MY SORRY ASS...

IT WAS A FANTASTIC SHOW. THE SWEDISH FANS WERE WONDERFUL.... I JUST WANTED WHAT I ORDERED EARLIER... THAT I DEMANDED AT THE PARTY... JACK DANIEL'S WITH A TEMPERATURE BETWEEN 10 AND 15 DEGREES CELSIUS.

AXL ROSE IS TAKEN INTO CUSTODY BY THE SWEDISH POLICE ON THE MORNING OF *TUESDAY JUNE 27TH* AFTER GETTING INTO A FIGHT WITH A HOTEL SECURITY GUARD.

OFFICER TOVE HÄGG TOLD THE LOCAL THE ROCK STAR WAS IN A CELL STILL DRUNK AT 11AM ON TUESDAY. SHE SAID HE IS BEING CHARGED WITH DAMAGING PROPERTY, ASSAULTING A SECURITY GUARD AND THREATENING POLICE IN THE SQUAD CAR ON THE WAY TO THE STATION.

AXL JOINED THE BAND AT AN AFTER SHOW AT CAFE OPERA AT 2:20AM AXL WAS IMMEDIATELY SURROUNDED BY A THRONG OF LEATHER-PRESSED BLONDE FEMALES AND SWEDISH CELEBRITIES, INCLUDING MEMBERS OF ACE OF BASE AND THE POODLES.

THE BAND HAD PREVIOUSLY ASKED TO BE MET BY SWEDISH BLONDES AT THE AFTER-PARTY... A REQUEST WHICH WAS PUBLICISED IN THE LOCAL MEDIA.

THE PARTY CONTINUED INTO THE EARLY HOURS OF THE MORNING AT THE BERNS HOTEL WHERE THE BAND IS STAYING... AND THEN SOMETHING WENT WRONG. AT 7:52AM AXL ROSE WAS ARRESTED AND BROUGHT TO THE POLICE STATION IN THE NORRMALM SECTION OF STOCKHOLM. THE HOTEL MANAGER, JOAKIM OLAUSON, CONFIRMED TO AFTONBLADET THAT THE ROCK STAR WAS INVOLVED IN A BRAWL AT THE HOTEL... "I CAN CONFIRM THAT THERE HAS BEEN AN INCIDENT IN WHICH AXL ROSE WAS INVOLVED. SINCE THIS IS AN ONGOING POLICE INVESTIGATION, I MUST REFER YOU TO THE POLICE."

FREDRIK NYLEN, ONE OF THE ARRESTING OFFICERS, TOLD AFTONBLADET THAT AXL ROSE WAS VERY AGGRESSIVE AND OUT OF CONTROL WHEN THE POLICE ARRIVED AT THE SCENE... SO MUCH SO THAT THE POLICE WERE FORCED TO HANDCUFF AND RESTRAIN HIM.

ACCORDING TO A WITNESS, AXL ROSE STARTED FIGHTING WITH A WOMAN. THE HOTEL STAFF TRIED TO INTERVENE AND THAT'S WHEN AXL WENT ON THE ATTACK.

A THIRTY-YEAR-OLD SECURITY GUARD, WHO BROKE UP THE FIGHT BETWEEN THE WOMAN AND ROSE, WAS BITTEN IN THE LEG AND TAKEN TO HOSPITAL FOR EVALUATION ON TUESDAY MORNING. "HE WAS TAKEN TO THE HOSPITAL THIS MORNING IN ORDER TO SEE IF THERE WAS ANY RISK OF HIM GETTING TETANUS," SAID ANTONIO SALLIENA, THE CHIEF OF THE PRIVATE SECURITY COMPANY EMPLOYING THE INJURED GUARD.

ACCORDING TO FREDRIK NYLEN, AXL'S ACTIONS DURING THE ARREST RESULTED IN ADDITIONAL CHARGES BEING FILED AGAINST HIM. "HE IS NOW ALSO SUSPECTED OF THREATENING AN OFFICER OF THE LAW," HE SAID. "THREATENING A POLICE OFFICER IS PUNISHABLE BY JAIL TIME, BUT IN THIS CASE IT WILL LIKELY RESULT IN A FINE."

ROSE WAS RELEASED FROM JAIL LATE TUESDAY AFTER CONFESSING TO THE CHARGES AND AGREEING TO PAY A FINE OF $5,500. OFFICIALS ALSO ORDERED ROSE TO PAY $1,300 IN DAMAGES TO THE SECURITY GUARD WHOM HE BIT ON THE LEG.

MY ASSISTANT BETA AND I WERE TALKING IN THE LOBBY OF THE HOTEL WHEN SECURITY STARTED TO GIVE US A HARD TIME... MY ONLY CONCERN WAS TO MAKE SURE SHE WAS OK.

STEVE ADLER WAS STRUGGLING TO GET CLEAN AND SOBER.

YEAH, I HAD A STROKE FROM COCAINE. I WAS SHOOTING IT. YOU WOULD THINK IT'D BE EASY TO KILL YOURSELF, BUT LET ME TELL YOU, IT'S NOT EASY... BUT YOU KNOW WHAT? NOTHING IS COOLER AND MORE ATTRACTIVE THAN A BIG COMEBACK, AND THAT'LL BE ME... THAT'S WHAT I'M WORKING ON NOW... I'M READY FOR IT!

SOMETIMES, IT CAN TAKE A FEW GO-ROUNDS ON THE ADDICTION TREADMILL... BUT HE WILL TRY THE OLD GAME AGAIN... FOR HE IS NOT HAPPY WITH HIS NEWFOUND SOBRIETY.

ADLER'S APPETITE

BE SOBER-MINDED; BE WATCHFUL. YOUR ADVERSARY THE DEVIL PROWLS AROUND LIKE A ROARING LION, SEEKING SOMEONE TO DEVOUR.

1 PETER 5:8

THE DEVIL, HE BIN WORKING HIS HOT ASS OVERTIME... ALL THE DISCORD CONTINUES... AND IT NEVER SHOWS ANY SIGN OF LETTING UP.

IN A RADIO INTERVIEW IN MAY ON INDIE 1031 FM'S CAMP FREDDY SHOW, SLASH TOLD HIS SIDE OF THE STORY...

YEAH, APPARENTLY IT'S BEEN REPORTED I PAID A NOCTURNAL VISIT TO AXL'S HOUSE... HIS MANAGEMENT SENT OUT A MEDIA STORY THAT I HAD GONE OVER THERE. THIS BLATANTLY FABRICATED THING THAT I'D GONE TO HIS HOUSE AND I SAID ALL THIS STUFF ABOUT MY BAND MATES... I THINK A LOT OF THIS WAS DONE TO PROMOTE THE NEXT GUNS RECORD AND TOUR. I HAVE NOT TALKED TO THE GUY SINCE 1996, SO IT'S GOING ON ELEVEN YEARS.

ON MARCH 6TH, GUNS N' ROSES FRONTMAN AXL ROSE RELEASED A STATEMENT TO THE MEDIA REGARDING THE LAWSUIT HE'D FILED DAYS BEFORE AGAINST SLASH... IN THE MISSIVE, ROSE TOOK SEVERAL SHOTS AT THE GUITARIST AND HIS VELVET REVOLVER BANDMATES: FORMER G N' R MEMBERS DUFF MCKAGAN AND MATT SORUM AND FORMER STONE TEMPLE PILOTS SINGER SCOTT WEILAND.

SCOTT WEILAND WAS NOT IN THE MOOD TO KEEP HIS THOUGHTS QUIET... HE PRACTICALLY HAD A SHIT FIT!

IN THE STATEMENT ISSUED THROUGH HIS MANAGEMENT TEAM, SANCTUARY GROUP, AXL ROSE CLAIMED THAT SLASH HAD TOLD HIM, "DUFF WAS SPINELESS, WEILAND WAS A FRAUD" AND THAT HE "HATES MATT SORUM." ROSE ADMONISHED SLASH AND DUFF FOR MAKING "NEGATIVE AND MALICIOUS STATEMENTS ABOUT HIM IN THE PRESS IN ORDER TO GARNER PUBLICITY" AS PART OF "A VINDICTIVE ATTEMPT TO AGGRANDISE THEIR OWN STATURE AND REWRITE HISTORY THROUGH FALSE STATEMENTS..."

ON FRIDAY, I POSTED TO THE VELVET REVOLVER WEBSITE AND THIS IS WHAT I SAID... GET IN THE RING... GO TO THE GYM, MOTHERFUCKER, OR IF YOU PREFER, GET A NEW WIG, MOTHERFUCKER... I THINK I'LL RESIST THE URGE TO 'STOOP' TO YOUR LEVEL. OH SHIT, HERE IT COMES, YOU FAT, BOTOX-FACED, WIG-WEARIN' FUCK! OKAY, I FEEL BETTER NOW... DON'T THINK FOR A SECOND WE DON'T KNOW WHERE THOSE WORDS CAME FROM. YOUR UNORIGINAL, UNCREATIVE LITTLE MIND, THE SAME MIND THAT HAD TO RELY ON ITS BANDMATES TO WRITE MELODIES AND LYRICS. WHO'S THE FRAUD NOW, BITCH? DAMN, I COULDN'T IMAGINE PEOPLE WRITING FOR ME. HOW MANY ALBUMS HAVE YOU PUT OUT, MAN, AND HOW LONG DID IT TAKE THE CURRENT CONFIGURATION OF THIS SO-CALLED 'BAND' TO MAKE THIS ALBUM? HOW LONG? AND WITHOUT THE ONLY GUYS THAT VALIDATED THE NAME. HOW DARE YOU? SHAME ON YOU! HOW DARE YOU CALL OUR BASS PLAYER 'SPINELESS'!? WE TOURED OUR ALBUM OVER A YEAR AND A HALF. HOW MANY SHOWS HAVE YOU PLAYED OVER THE LAST TEN YEARS? OH, THAT'S RIGHT, YOU BAILED OUT ON YOUR LONG-AWAITED COMEBACK TOUR, LEAVING YOUR REMAINING FANS FEELING, SHALL WE SAY, A TRIFLE MIFFED? I WON'T EVEN LIST WHAT I'VE ACCOMPLISHED BECAUSE I DON'T NEED TO... WHAT WE'RE TALKING ABOUT HERE IS A FRIGHTENED LITTLE MAN WHO ONCE THOUGHT HE WAS KING, BUT UNFORTUNATELY THIS KING WITHOUT HIS COURT IS NOTHING BUT A MEMORY OF THE ASSHOLE HE ONCE WAS.

AXL AND GUNS N' ROSES WERE GEARING UP FOR THE GREAT DAY AT LONG LAST. AFTER YEARS OF RUMOUR, COUNTER-RUMOUR AND ENDLESS INTRIGUE... ON OCTOBER 22ND 2008 THE TITLE TRACK AND FIRST SINGLE FROM CHINESE DEMOCRACY IS RELEASED TO RADIO WORLDWIDE AT 6AM EASTERN TIME. LATER THAT SAME DAY, THE ALBUM'S RELEASE DATE IS ANNOUNCED... THE LONG AWAITED BEHEMOTH HAS FINALLY WASHED UP ON THE RETAIL SHORES OF AMERICA.

THE ALBUM FEATURES FIVE GUITAR PLAYERS AND A RUMOURED APPEARANCE BY BRIAN MAY...

RECORDED IN OVER FOURTEEN STUDIOS...

WITH THE AFOREMENTIONED MOBY AND YOUTH AS PRODUCERS. EVENTUALLY THE ALBUM WAS RE-RECORDED BY ROY THOMAS BAKER, THE UBER PRODUCER OF JOURNEY, THE CARS, QUEEN AND MORE...

AS WELL AS PRODUCTION CREDITS FOR CARAM COSTANZO AND AXL ROSE.

ALMOST FIFTEEN YEARS IN THE MAKING, CHINESE DEMOCRACY WAS FINALLY RELEASED... DESPITE THE RESOUNDING HOOPLA AROUND ITS COMPLETION, THE ALBUM FAILED TO MAKE A SUBSTANTIAL CHART IMPACT. IT PEAKED AT NUMBER TWO IN THE UK AND NUMBER THREE IN THE USA... WITH THE FIRST SINGLE ONLY RISING AS HIGH AS NUMBER TWENTY-SEVEN...

IN THE UK'S CLASSIC ROCK REVIEW OF CHINESE DEMOCRACY, WRITER JON HOTTEN CONCLUDED: "THIS RECORD IS THE SOUND OF NO ONE SAYING NO TO AXL ROSE FOR FOURTEEN YEARS... IT MAY NEVER BE AS LOVED AS APPETITE FOR DESTRUCTION BUT DECADES FROM NOW PEOPLE WILL STILL ASSEMBLE AROUND IT AND STARE UP AT ITS BAROQUE FACADE, CONFIDENT THAT WE WON'T SEE ITS LIKE TOO OFTEN... IF AT ALL".

JON PARELES, WRITING FOR THE NEW YORK TIMES, OPINED: "CHINESE DEMOCRACY IS AN ALBUM THAT IS GRANDIOSE, OVERWROUGHT, OVERBLOWN, SUPERFLUOUS AND HAS OCCASIONALLY THE GREATEST SONGS ROSE HAS RECORDED TO DATE..."

To: The Rock And Roll Hall Of Fame,
Guns N' Roses Fans and Whom It May Concern,

When the nominations for the Rock And Roll Hall Of Fame were first announced I had mixed emotions but, in an effort to be positive, wanting to make the most of things for the fans and with their enthusiasm, I was honored, excited and hoped that somehow this would be a good thing. Of course I realized as things stood, if Guns N' Roses were to be inducted it'd be somewhat of a complicated or awkward situation. Since then we've listened to fans, talked with members of the board of the Hall Of Fame, communicated with and read various public comments and jabs from former members of Guns N' Roses, had discussions with the president of the Hall Of Fame, read various press (some legit, some contrived) and read other artist's comments weighing in publicly on Guns and the Hall with their thoughts. Under the circumstances I feel we've been polite, courteous, and open to an amicable solution in our efforts to work something out. Taking into consideration the history of Guns N' Roses, those who plan to attend along with those the Hall, for reasons of their own, have chosen to include in "our" induction (that for the record are decisions I don't agree with, support or feel the Hall has any right to make), and how (albeit no easy task) those involved with the Hall have handled things... no offense meant to anyone but the Hall Of Fame Induction Ceremony doesn't appear to be somewhere I'm actually wanted or respected. For the record, I would not begrudge anyone from Guns their accomplishments or recognition for such. Neither I or anyone in my camp has made any requests or demands of the Hall Of Fame. It's their show not mine. That said, I won't be attending The Rock And Roll Hall Of Fame Induction 2012 Ceremony and I respectfully decline my induction as a member of Guns N' Roses to the Rock And Roll Hall Of Fame. I strongly request that I not be inducted in absentia and please know that no one is authorized nor may anyone be permitted to accept any induction for me or speak on my behalf. Neither former members, label representatives nor the Rock And Roll Hall Of Fame should imply whether directly, indirectly or by omission that I am included in any purported induction of "Guns N' Roses". This decision is personal. This letter is to help clarify things from my and my camp's perspective. Neither is meant to offend, attack or condemn. Though unfortunately I'm sure there will be those who take offense (God knows how long I'll have to contend with the fallout), I certainly don't intend to disappoint anyone, especially the fans, with this decision. Since the announcement of the nomination we've actively sought out a solution to what, with all things considered, appears to be a no win, at least for me, "damned if I do, damned if I don't" scenario all the way around.

In regard to a reunion of any kind of either the Appetite or Illusion lineups, I've publicly made myself more than clear. Nothing's changed. The only reason, whether under the circumstances, in my opinion at this point, under the guise of "for the fans" or whatever justification of the moment, for anyone to continue to ask, suggest or demand a reunion are misguided attempts to distract from our efforts with our current lineup of myself, Dizzy Reed, Tommy Stinson, Frank Ferrer, Richard Fortus, Chris Pitman, Ron "Bumblefoot" Thal and DJ Ashba. Izzy came out with us a few times back in '06 and I invited him to join us at our LA Forum show last year. Steven was at our show at the Hard Rock, later in '06 in Las Vegas, where I invited him to our after-party and was rewarded with his subsequent interviews filled with reunion lies. Lesson learned. Duff joined us in 2010 and again in '11 along with his band, Loaded, opening in Seattle and Vancouver. For me, with the exception of Izzy or Duff joining us on stage if they were so inclined somewhere in the future for a song or two, that's enough. There's a seemingly endless amount of revisionism and fantasies out there for the sake of self-promotion and business opportunities masking the actual realities. Until every single one of those generating from or originating with the earlier lineups has been brought out in the light, there isn't room to consider a conversation let alone a reunion. Maybe if it were you it'd be different. Maybe you'd do it for this reason or that. Peace, whatever. I love our band now. We're there for each other when the going get's rough. We love our fans and work to give them every ounce of energy and heart we can. So let sleeping dogs lie or lying dogs sleep or whatever. Time to move on. People get divorced. Life doesn't owe you your own personal happy ending, especially at another's, or in this case several others', expense. But hey if ya gotta then maybe we can get the "no show, grandstanding, publicity stunt, disrespectful, he doesn't care about the fans" crap out of the way as quickly as we can and let's move on. No one's taking the ball and going home. Don't get it twisted. For more than a decade and a half we've endured the double standards, the greed of this industry and the ever present seemingly limitless supply of wannabes and unscrupulous, irresponsible media types. Not to imply anything in this particular circumstance, but from my perspective in regard to both the Hall and a reunion, the ball's never been in our court.
In closing, regardless of this decision and as hard to believe or as ironic as it may seem, I'd like to sincerely thank the board for their nomination and their votes for Guns' induction. More importantly I'd like to thank the fans for being there over the years, making any success we've had possible and for enjoying and supporting Guns N' Roses music. I wish the Hall a great show, congratulations to all the other artists being inducted and to our fans we look forward to seeing you on tour!!

Sincerely,

Axl Rose

P.S. P.S.

ON APRIL 14TH, 2012 IN CLEVELAND, OHIO AND IN FRONT OF 9,000 FANS...
THE SHOW WENT ON WITHOUT AXL AND WITH MYLES KENNEDY TAKING THE
LEAD VOCALS SLOT. IZZY HAD DECLINED TO BE THERE TOO, BUT MORE QUIETLY...

BILLIE JOE ARMSTRONG FROM
GREEN DAY RECALLED THE FIRST
TIME HE SAW THE BAND ON MTV:
"I THOUGHT, ONE OF THESE GUYS
COULD END UP DEAD OR IN JAIL...
IT'S THE BEST DEBUT ALBUM IN
THE HISTORY OF ROCK 'N' ROLL.
EVERY SONG HITS HARD... IT TAKES
YOU ON A TRIP TO THE SEEDY
WORLD OF LOS ANGELES... THE
THING THAT SET THEM APART
FROM EVERYONE ELSE WAS GUTS...
THEY NEVER LOST THEIR EDGE
FOR ONE SECOND."

LET'S SEE, WHO
AM I MISSING?

HERE IS THE MISSING MAN... THE ONE WHO ALL THESE
CHANGES OCCURRED AROUND. AXL MADE HIS FIRST
APPEARANCE ON TV IN YEARS... OCTOBER 24TH 2012
ON THE JIMMY KIMMEL SHOW. AXL SAYS HE HAS A
PLAQUE IN HIS HOUSE... PUNCTUALITY IS THE THIEF
OF TIME... BUT AXL MADE THE SHOW ON TIME AND
SEEMED TO BE ON HIS BEST BEHAVIOUR.

PERLA HUDSON, THE WIFE
OF EX-LEAD GUITARIST
SLASH, TOLD US WEEKLY,
AS SHE TUNED IN FOR THE
OCTOBER 24TH TELECAST...

PUNCTUALITY
IS THE THIEF
OF TIME?

IT'S AN
OSCAR WILDE
QUOTE.

WHAT
TIME WILL
YOU GUYS
REALLY
GO ON?

PROBABLY
WHAT TIME
WE'RE SUPPOSED
TO... AS SOON AS I
FIND OUT WHAT
THAT IS.

I WAS
WAITING
FOR SOMETHING
ENLIGHTENING AND ALL
I GOT WAS A PROMOTION
FOR A SHOW... AND HIS
EVIDENT AFFINITY FOR A
CHILI BURGER. WHERE IS THE
LOVE, AXL? AND I STAYED UP
FOR THIS? SEX, DRUGS AND
CHILI DOGS... LONG LIVE
AXL ROSE... AND A
HALLOWEEN
TREE...

HE'S HAD
A SLASH, A
BUCKETHEAD
AND A BUMBLEFOOT
AND EVIDENTLY WAY
TOO MANY TOMMY'S
CHILI BURGERS... HOPE
THERE WERE SOME
LEFT FOR THE
AUDIENCE...

Guns N' Roses   Gallery

At the time I really loved this cover, but I think the top guy called it right. Too much going on to work as a cover.

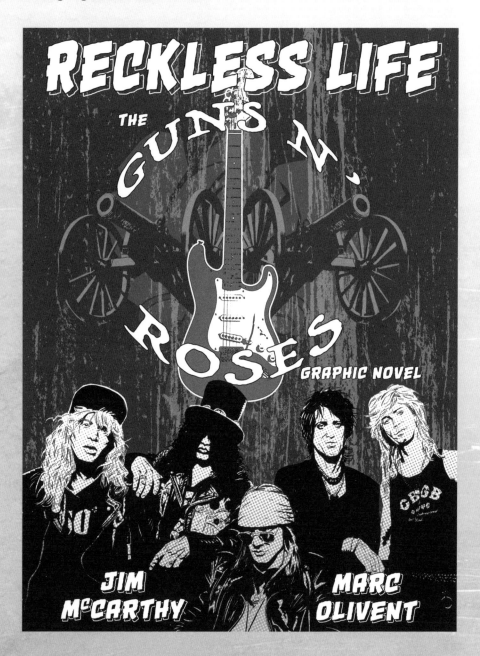

Guns N' Roses   Gallery

As we couldn't use the official Guns N' Roses logo, I decided to come up with my own. I thought using actual guns (or pistols) would just look derivative of the original so I went for some proper guns!!!

Guns N' Roses   Gallery

This was produced just to see what the band would look like if I drew them. Once I'd done it, I was pretty happy to carry the style forward into the book. Duff looks awesome!! Actually, he *is* awesome!

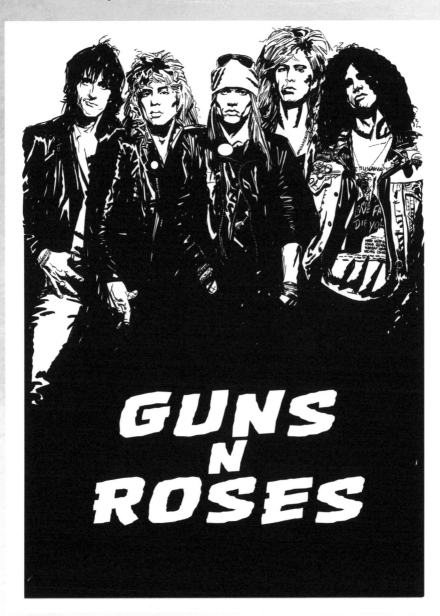

Guns N' Roses Gallery

And this was to check what an actual page from the strip might look like. We wanted to get a feel for how everything might mesh together (or not) and see what would happen when I tried to draw the guys in a sequential narrative. Turned out okay, I think, and it gave me the belief that I could actually pull this off!

Jim McCarthy

Jim McCarthy's career in publishing began with 2000AD and work on *Bad Company*, *Bix Barton*, *The Grudgefather*, *Kyd Cyborg* and *Judge Dredd*.

He has also immersed himself in American music forms and culture, resulting in *Voices Of Latin Rock*, which was published by Hal Leonard. It is the first book to examine Santana, Latin rock culture and the Mission District, the area where this nascent political and musical art form emerged. This is one of the radical birth points of Hispanic music, art and culture.

Voices Of Latin Rock led to a series of concerts in San Francisco promoting autism awareness and which featured Carlos Santana, Booker T, Los Lobos, Sly Stone, George Clinton, El Chicano, Malo, Taj Mahal and The Doobie Brothers, among others.

Jim is also engaged in producing insightful, contemporary graphic novels, linked to music subjects. The most recent was *Metallica: Nothing Else Matters*. Other graphic biographies have covered The Sex Pistols, Kurt Cobain, Tupac Shakur, Eminem, Michael Jackson, The Ramones and Bob Marley.

"You can do whatever you want within a graphic novel. You can be very cinematic and put things in that you couldn't in a traditional biography, and maybe not even in a film. You can come at it from different angles, different tenses, different points-of-view. You can use visual symbols to make a lot of comments in a single panel. When it comes to televised music documentaries, they seem to follow a prescribed path. I try to approach each one in a different way."

Jim McCarthy

Marc Olivent

Marc Olivent is a freelance illustrator based in Lincoln. He specialises in comic book illustration, a passion he developed at a very early age by reading (and re-reading and re-reading...) Seventies and Eighties Stan Lee-created Marvel comics. From those early days, Marc knew exactly where his career path lie (although it took a little longer to get there than he first envisaged).

He never stopped reading comics and would study the visual storytelling techniques employed by the masters of the craft. His influences are many, but his style is all his own (be that a good or bad thing!).

Previous work includes Dark Horse Presents strip 'Sundown Crossroads', 'Rick Fury' and 'Zezi' for Rok comics and *Dark Satanic Mills* for Walker books, on which he worked with legendary comics illustrator John Higgins (*Watchmen*, *Judge Dredd*). *Dark Satanic Mills* was nominated for the 2015 Kate Greenaway award for illustration.

Reckless Life The Guns N'Roses Graphic Novel is his first book for Omnibus Press with writer and 2000AD alumni Jim McCarthy.

METALLICA:
NOTHING ELSE MATTERS
JIM McCARTHY & BRIAN WILLIAMSON

Brian Williamson's dramatic artwork and Jim McCarthy's razor-sharp script capture
all the excitement and traumas of thrash metal's most successful band. From their
initial underground success to commercial triumphs that include *The Black Album*,
nine Grammys and a total of over 100 million albums sold worldwide, *Metallica:
Nothing Else Matters* is a thrilling roller-coaster ride spanning two decades of highs
and lows on the road and in the studio.

Available from all good bookshops

or in case of difficulty www.omnibuspress.com